Prosecutors' Forensic Speech in Implicit Pragmalinguistics

Prosecutors' Forensic Speech in Implicit Pragmalinguistics

By

Irina Zyubina

CAMBRIDGE SCHOLARS PUBLISHING

Prosecutors' Forensic Speech in Implicit Pragmalinguistics,
by Irina Zyubina

This book first published 2011

Cambridge Scholars Publishing

12 Back Chapman Street, Newcastle upon Tyne, NE6 2XX, UK

British Library Cataloguing in Publication Data
A catalogue record for this book is available from the British Library

ISBN (10): 1-4438-2961-7, ISBN (13): 978-1-4438-2961-8

TABLE OF CONTENTS

Part I **1**
Forensic Speech of a Prosecutor
1. Forensic speech of a prosecutor as a speech genre
2. Individual speech behavior of prosecutors from the point of view of pragmalinguistics
3. Stereotyped speech behavior of prosecutors from the point of view of pragmalinguistics
4. Methods of studying the speech behavior of public prosecutors in Implicit Pragmalinguistics

Part II **29**
***Individual* Speech Behavior of Prosecutors of English-speaking and Russian-speaking Lingua-cultural Communities in Implicit Pragmalinguistics**
1. Requirements for the linguistic analysis in Implicit Pragmalinguistics
2. *Russian-speaking* prosecutors' speech behavior in different periods of history and laying before different addressees
   2.1. Russian-speaking prosecutors' speech behavior at the end of the XIX century in laying before a trial by jury
   2.2. Russian-speaking prosecutors' speech behavior in the USSR in 20s - 40s years of the XX century in laying before a professional trial
   2.3. Russian-speaking prosecutors' speech behavior at the beginning of the XXI century
      2.3.1. Russian-speaking prosecutors' speech behavior at the beginning of the XXI century in laying before a professional trial
      2.3.2. Russian-speaking prosecutors' speech behavior at the beginning of the XXI century in laying before a trial by jury
3. *English-speaking* prosecutors' speech behavior at the beginning of the XXI century in laying before a trial by jury

Part III **69**
Comparative Analysis of *Stereotyped* Speech Behavior of Prosecutors
1. Comparative analysis of stereotyped speech behavior of Russian-speaking prosecutors in different periods of history
   1.1. Comparative analysis of stereotyped speech behavior of Russian-speaking prosecutors in laying before a trial by jury in the XIX century and in the XXI century
   1.2. Comparative analysis of stereotyped speech behavior of Russian-speaking prosecutors in laying before a professional trial in 20s - 40s years of the XX century and at the beginning of the XXI century
2. Comparative analysis of stereotyped speech behavior of Russian-speaking prosecutors in laying before different addressees
3. Comparative analysis of stereotyped speech behavior of prosecutors belonging to different lingua-cultural communities (Russian-speaking and English-speaking)

Conclusion 83

Appendix 85

Works Cited 99

List of the Speeches 109

PART I

FORENSIC SPEECH OF A PROSECUTOR

1. Forensic speech of a prosecutor as a speech genre

The purpose of this opening section is to determine the features of stereotyped speech behaviour of public prosecutors in the speech genre of "speech for the prosecution." To identify these peculiarities, it is first important to determine the status of this speech genre.

In modern linguistics, there is no generally accepted concept of a speech genre. There are many definitions of the term "genre" (Dementiev 1997, 109). In our study, we follow Bakhtin, who defines speech genres as relatively stable types of utterances, produced by the areas of language use. Three things—thematic content, style and compositional structure—are inextricably linked in a statement and are identified by the specifics of each sphere of communication (Bakhtin 1986, 428). From the point of view of linguapragmatics, a speech genre is a text produced in a typical situation of communication and reproduced in the communicative activity of native speakers. It is characterised by a certain set of elements of the situation, as well as by a set of speech tasks undertaken (Nazarov 1997, 22).

The main difference between one genre and another is not in linguistic features, although each of the genres is characterised by the predominance, or, conversely, the absence of certain linguistic elements, but in the content orientation of a text and its functional purpose (Bushev n.d.).

The concept of Bakhtin distinguishes primary (simple) and secondary (complex) speech genres. Secondary speech genres—novels, plays, research, great journalistic genres, etc.—appear in more complex and highly developed organised cultural communication (primarily written), i.e. fiction, scientific, socio-political, etc. In the course of their formation, they absorb and use various primary genres (for example, a phrase of everyday dialogue) appearing in conditions of spontaneous speech communication (Bakhtin 1986, 430).

The speech for the prosecution in court is a secondary speech genre. It can be referred to as a type of oral public speech which sharply differs from everyday speech and which is characterised by the following set of features:

(1) there is one speaker and many listeners
(2) the change of roles between "speaker" and "listener" is not possible
(3) the relationships between the speaker and listeners are official, and they are characterised by inequality of the roles in the act of communication
(4) the theme is fixed (Golanova 1993, 137).

Originally, the prosecutor's speech existed as an oral speech, and after this came to us in the form of printed text. Because of this fact, paralinguistic intensifiers such as voice timbre, character and strength of pronunciation (whisper, shout), facial expressions, gestures, body movements and extralinguistic sensitisers disappear (Kisseleva 1978, 113). In addition, the psychic ground of speech perception, environment, the social roles of the participants of the speech act, authoritativeness, and the speaker's appearance, which are clearly present in oral speech and amplify the positive effect of the speaker's influence, also disappear (Varnavskikh 2001, 179). The speech of a public prosecutor is represented as a text, and in an analysis of any text which is a part of a joint practice of people, of processes of interpersonal interaction, the pragmatic intention, or function, of the text is taken into account (Najer 1990, 5).

A forensic speech performs a number of interconnected functions: cognition, communication and psychological impact (Enikeev 1996, 561). A functional style stands in relation to a speech genre as its peculiar systemic manifestation. A functional style in a speech genre is manifested in the form of a purposeful selection of certain linguistic devices and techniques. A speech genre in relation to a style serves as its concrete application in various situations of communication in a definite sphere of activity. A genre is not considered to be the equivalent to the concept of "style," but a separate concept concurrently parallel and relative to "style" (Drugaliova 2003, 253).

At the present stage of scientific development, one of the major problems of stylistics is the classification of functional styles. Despite a large number of recent papers devoted to functional styles, there is still no consensus on the number existing. Different sources give contradictory numbers: three (Piotrovskiy 1960, 20–21), five (Matveeva 1997, 21–25), eight (Gvozdev 1965, 17–28) and as many as twelve (Cheremissin 1971, 95–96). Both the number and characteristics of functional styles are different in the classifications of different researchers. It is advisable to select styles, not so much on theoretic but on pragmatic grounds (Puzyriov 1997, 7), and it is on pragmatic grounds that we distinguish five styles: an official style, a publicistic style, a scientific style, a colloquial style and a belles-lettres or fiction style.

A forensic speech as an oratory genre has its own stylistic originality (Mikhailov 1968; Pirinova 2001). This peculiarity is demonstrated by the following: firstly, a forensic speech refers to two styles of literary language, publicistic and official, and secondly reflects features of other styles of literary language, scientific and colloquial. Thus, the speech genre of speech for the prosecution is a complex functional-style formation which uses the signs of different functional styles. Let us study in more detail the manifestation of the features of listed styles (publicistic, official, scientific and colloquial) in the speech genre of speech for the prosecution.

First, we will analyse a speech of a public prosecutor from the point of view of the publicistic functional style and study the manifestation of the main feature of this style—the use of the open evaluation for best effect—in the speech for the prosecution. The main goal of the publicistic style is to influence a listener or a reader for agitation and propaganda. Thus, for example, a public prosecutor of the former Soviet Union had the task not only of creating around a crime and a defendant an atmosphere of condemnation, but also to be an advocate of communist ethics and morality (Baskov 1977, 161). Before each public prosecutor in any socio-political system, there is the goal of creating an atmosphere of conviction around a criminal, and is why each episode of a crime is reviewed and evaluated from this perspective. The speech of a public prosecutor has a bright negative character, both from the point of view of a negative component (the average speech-genre index of negative evaluation is 45 percent, whereas the positive is only 12 percent; see table 7) and from the point of view of the diversity of expression.

Designations of negative are also more differentiated than the positive in speeches of other kinds. This position is based on the studies of cognitive psychology, according to which the information associated with something unpleasant for a person, with negative emotions, is more differentiated than the information with positive connotations. According to psychologists, a person distinguishes in more detail what is causing their discomfort and differentiates unpleasant emotions better than pleasant ones (Volf 1986, 102).

An explicit expression of the negative attitude of an author may be made on the basis of invectives. An invective, through semantics, expressive colour and evaluative content, communicates the intention of the speaker or writer to humiliate, insult, dishonour or disgrace an addressee or third person in a sharp and cynical form, as much as possible (Bazylev n.d.). In modern Russia and Britain, there is no invective vocabulary in the statements of prosecutors speaking in court, but such a vocabulary is very characteristic for the public prosecutors of the USSR working in the 1920s to 1940s, and to a lesser extent in the speeches for the prosecution working at the end of the nineteenth century in Russia.

Invective vocabulary in the speeches for the prosecution is so diverse that one can divide it into the following types according to the principle of direct/indirect nomination (category):

I. Direct nomination:

(a) Invective vocabulary originally denoting a person engaged in anti-social, socially condemned activities (translations of the examples are in brackets following the examples):

(1) *Хохлов—**преступник*** [Khokhlov is **a criminal**] (Pokrovskiy 1965, 153)
(2) *Инглинк говорил, / что таких **рвачей** надо терпеть* [Inglink said / one should bear such **grabbers**] (Kondrushkin 1965, 467–468)
(3) *Троцкисты и правые – это **капитулянты*** [Trotskyists and right-wingers are **trucklers**] (Vyshinskiy 1955, 325)
(4) *Кровью пионера обагрены руки правых **изменников**.* [The hands of the right-wing **traitors** became stained with blood of the pioneer] (Pokrovskiy 1965, 15)

(b) These words have a bright negative connotation which is the main component of the meaning but in a specific time frame:

(5) *Они хотели вернуть **кулаков** и **помещиков**,/ действуя единым фронтом с **фашистами*** [They wanted to return the **"kulaks"** (**rich peasants**) and **landlords** / acting as a united front with the <u>fascists</u>] (Pokrovskiy 1965, 11–12)
(6) *Ни один сколько-нибудь серьезный заговор против Советской власти в СССР не обошелся без прямого и самого активного участия в нем **иностранных капиталистов**.* [None of any serious plots against the Soviet regime in the Soviet Union was without the direct and very

active participation of **foreign capitalists**] (Vyshinskiy 1955, 250)

(c) Invective words containing in their meanings a negative evaluation, and, what is more, a very expressive evaluation of someone's personality:

(7) *Они вдохновляли силы кулачества и других* ***подонков*** *общества.* [They inspired the forces of the kulaks and other **dregs** of society] (Pokrovskiy 1965, 13)
(8) *Русскому обществу нужно знать разоблаченную на суде правду об этой* ***заразе.*** [The Russian society should know the unmasked court truth about this **plague**] (Muraviov, 25)

II. Indirect nomination:

(a) Metaphors referring to the names of animals, birds, insects, which cause unpleasant associations for the listeners:

(9) *Партия эсеров превратилась в* ***змею,*** */ жалящую в пяту* [The Socialist Revolutionary Party has turned into a **snake,** / stinging the heel] (Pokrovskiy 1965, 200–201)
(10) *Седков оставил такой сладкий кусок, / что в нем увязли все* ***слетевшиеся*** *им попользоваться.* [Sedkov had left such a sweet piece, / that all **those flying together** stuck in it] (Koni 1968, 407–408)

Here (in the 10th example) we can see a hint at a fly as a kind of insects

(11) *В декабре Рыков* ***каркает*** *о непрочности Советской власти.* [In December Rykov **croaks** about the fragility of the Soviet power] (Vyshinskiy 1955, 484)

In this example we cannot but feel the attempt of the public prosecutor to show us Rykov as a bird, a crow.

(12) Эта ***мышь,/*** *пойманная в мышеловку* … [This **mouse,** / caught with a trap …] (Vyshinskiy 1955, 843–844)
(13) *Бухарин – это проклятая* ***помесь лисицы и свиньи*** [Bukharin is a damn **cross between a fox and a pig**] (Vyshinskiy 1955, 478)

(b) Occasional (especially created) formations have the aim of humiliating or insulting an addressee:

(14) *После крушения* ***учредилки*** (то есть “Учредительное собрание”) *эсеры могли заняться пропагандой своих идей в массах.* [After the collapse of the **“uchredilka”** (“Constituent Assembly”) socialist revolutionaries could promote their ideas to the masses] (Pokrovskiy 1965, 42)
(15) *Оцените роль этого господинчика, / болтающего о том, / что* ***обер-бандит*** *и англо-германский шпион Троцкий уже в 1932 году сбросил свой* ***“левацкий мундир.”*** [Evaluate the role of this gentleman, / chatting / that the **“ober-bandit”** (“subaltern bandit”) and the Anglo-German spy Trotsky had already thrown off his **“levatskiy mundir”** (this is a new expression for a uniform of the left-wing party) in 1932.] (Vyshinskiy 1955, 70–72)
(16) *Бухарин—****патентованный лицемер и иезуит****.* [Bukharin is a **patented hypocrite and Jesuit**] (Vyshinskiy 1955, 765)

(c) The names of literary characters and their forms which have a negative characterisation:

(17) *Тот самый Вандервельде—это* ***Чичиков*** *с его мертвыми душами.* [The very Vandervelde is **Chichikov** with his dead souls] (Lunacharskiy 1965, 423)

This literary character (Chichikov) is from the famous *Miortviye dushi* (*Dead Souls*) by Gogol

(18) *Меня мало интересует* ***хлестаковщина*** *Окладского.* [I am not so much interested in **“khlestakovshchina”** of Okladskiy] (Koni 1968, 221)

“Khlestakovshchina” is a word made of the name Ivan Alexandrovich Khlestakov, the main character of Gogol’s *The Government Inspector*.

(d) Proper names with deliberate changing of the number (singular into the plural), claiming to be a generalisation and reinforcing the negative assessment of the defendant and his crime:

(19) ***Бухарины*** *и* ***Рыковы, Ягоды*** *и* ***Булановы, Крестинские*** *и* ***Розенгольцы, Икрамовы, Шаранговичи, Ходжаевы*** *под руководством Троцкого делают свое черное дело …* [**Bukharins** and **Rykovs, Yagodas** and **Bulanovs, Krestinskies** and **Rosengoltzes, Ikramovs, Sharangoviches, Khodjaevs** under the leadership of Trotsky do their dirty work …] (Vyshinskiy 1955, 114)

(20) *Тогда вслед за* ***Окладскими*** *прошли* ***Дегаевы.*** [Then after **Okladskies** there were **Degayevs**.]. (Koni 1968, 690)

(21) *А у эсеров* ***полковники Галкины*** *стояли во главе армии. /* ***Колчаки, чаплины*** *взяли в железные руки партию эсеров.* [And the Socialist Revolutionary Party had **Generals Galkins** standing at the head of the army./**Kolchaks, Chaplins** took into their iron hands the Socialist Revolutionary Party.] (Lunacharskiy 1965, 509 and 616)

The analysis of the expression of the negative evaluation with the help of invective vocabulary shows that this phenomenon is a characteristic of "totalitarian linguistic consciousness" (Vorozhbitova 2000, 10). However, at the present stage of the development of Russian and British societies in the era of democratic changes, this method of impact on a listener is not acceptable.

Use of a large number of high and solemn words by the public prosecutor also serves for the formation of evaluation as a way of influencing:

(22) … *человек, / который сейчас не испытывает никаких* ***угрызений совести*** */ и боится только* ***справедливого возмезди*** … [… a man,/who is not **conscience-stricken** now/and is afraid of only **just retribution** …] (Trukhanov 1985, 716–718)

(23) *Пора сорвать маску с этих непрошеных* ***благодетелей человечества***. [It is time to tear the mask from these uninvited **benefactors of mankind**.] (Muraviov, 18)

(24) *Троцкизм и правые превратились в* ***оруженосцев*** *буржуазной контрреволюции* [Trotskyism and the right-wing party became the **sword-bearers** of the bourgeois counter-revolution] (Vyshinskiy 1955, 352)

The publicistic style is also characterised by the use of the words on social, political and ethical themes:

(25) ***тайное сообщество, правительство, злодеяние*** [**secret society**, **government**, **evil deed**] (Muraviov, 7, 13, 3)

In the speech for the prosecution one can see emotionally coloured words, typical for the publicistic functional style:

(26) ***отголоски того мирка, скромненький офицер с капитальцем*** [***echoes of that "microcosm," a "modestish" officer with a "kapitalets"*** [that is a very small amount of money] (Koni 1968, 24 and 43)

(27) *В этом* ***вихре*** *поднимается много и* ***мути.*** [In this **whirlwind** a lot of **turbidity** rises] (Lunacharskiy 1965, 133)

As we can see, there is an abundance of high and solemn words, lexemes on social, political, moral and ethical themes and emotionally coloured words in prosecution speeches before the professional trial in the Soviet period, and before the jury in all periods.

Each court indictment in every state system or regime is a public political statement. A state prosecutor always acts not on their behalf, as the others members of the trial, but on behalf of the state and the law. The specific purpose of the prosecution speech is to convince the court and all other addressees in the courtroom of the defendant's guilt, to make them agree with the conclusions offered by the prosecutor, and thereby to facilitate the proper formation of internal judicial opinions and legal consciousness of citizens. Through their speech, a public prosecutor helps to create an atmosphere of moral condemnation around the criminal and mobilises public opinion against crime. Pleading in court stimulates thought, and is therefore an important means of influence, and the formation of the listeners' certain worldview, social and political consciousness is one more feature of the publicistic style. Therefore, the speech genre of prosecution speech can be considered the publicistic functional style of modern language.

The following functional style that the speech genre of prosecution speech should be described is the official style, characterised by accuracy and standardisation of expression. Let us analyse how these features are manifested in a court speech of a public prosecutor.

Speeches of the participants in the judicial debate are carried out in the legal field, serving the official relationship between justice and the defendant, and determine the position of the supervisory bodies of the state in a particular case. Therefore, an important social function of a judiciary speech allows us to speak about its correlation with the official style, primarily characterised by extreme accuracy, not allowing for another point of view. A judicial speaker, analysing the facts of the case, has no right to make a mistake to avoid the wrong determination of the court. Every phrase, every word must completely convey the point of view of the speaker (Ivakina 1995, 41–42). It is typical of the official style to use the words in their literal sense, and the system of speech here is, to a large extent, codified, so it is associated with the standardisation of the expression (Matveeva 1997, 22). Socially fixed formulas expressing legal relations definitely convey relevant concepts and facts. Let us give some examples: "legal action," "jurisdiction of a court," "principal suspect," "direct/material evidence," "attendant circumstances," and so on. Such expressions are found in any speech of a public prosecutor. The meaning of a legal cliché is fixed in legal documents and does not allow ambiguities. The terms of communication in an official sphere determine the appearance of standards. As everything in all legal relations is regulated, and communication is carried out according to certain standards which make this interaction easier, so speech standards turn out to be necessary and even desirable and justified. That is why there is an abundance of stable combinations of terminology (without emotion and expressivity) (Antonenko 1999, 152).

From the point of view of syntax, we can see that complex sentences with various types of causal relations, homogeneous parts of the sentence and participle constructions are used in official language of the speech for the prosecution. Subordinate conjunctions ("as," "because of," etc.), as well as parenthetical words are also commonly used ("first of all," "therefore," etc.) (Matveeva 1997, 22).

More often, the official style is used for naming the elements of the *corpus delicti*, the legal procedure, procedural documents and for drawing conclusions about the factual circumstances of the case and the punishment (Ivakina 1995, 44).

The official style is characterised by the "dryness" of presentation and by the lack of expressive means (Vvedenskaya 1994, 35), and more frequently exactness and laconism are observed in the prosecution speeches before professional judges at the present moment.

We have discussed how the official style is manifested in texts of the speech genre of prosecution speeches. Now let us turn to the scientific functional style.

With regard to the scientific functional style, all researchers identify such features as clearness of expression of thought, and a strong following of the norms and terms (Senkevich 1976, 36). For example:

(28) *Прошу квалифицировать данное деяние по статье 213.3 УК РФ как хулиганство, / т.е. грубое нарушение общественного порядка, / выражающее явное неуважение к обществу,/с применением насилия к гражданам, / совершенное с применением предметов, / используемых в качестве оружия.* [I ask you to qualify this act according to Article 213.3 of the Criminal Code of the Russian Federation as hooliganism, / that is a gross violation of public order / expressing a clear disrespect for society / with the use of violence to citizens, / committed with the use of objects / used as a weapon] (Glyuzitskiy, 23–27).

Scientific speech has inherent logical accuracy, objectivity and consistency (Razinkina 1972, 28), these traits helping it to be methodologically convincing (Volodina, n.d.). This consistency is seen in the composition of prosecution speech in court, consisting of the following parts (Enikeev 1996, 571–572):

(1) Opening statement
(2) Exposition of the factual circumstances of the act, the course of events of the case
(3) Analysis and evaluation of collected evidence of the case
(4) Argumentation of determination the nature of the crime
(5) Characteristics of the defendant and the victim
(6) Proposals for the sentence or the verdict
(7) Issues of compensation for the offense caused
(8) Analysis of the causes and conditions that contributed to the offence. Proposals to eliminate them
(9) Conclusion

The features and language means of the scientific style are most often seen in such parts as "Analysis and evaluation of collected evidence of the case" and "Argumentation of determination the nature of the crime." The main goal of the scientific style is proof, and the main features arising from the abstraction and accuracy of thought are generalisation and emphasised logical consistency of presentation, when the dynamics of thinking develop from the statement of the criminal acts to disprove the opposing point of view. Judgments and conclusions follow one after the other in strict logical sequence (Ivakina 1995, 44), especially if there is an absence of direct evidence of defendant's guilt and the prosecution is based on circumstantial evidence. Then the speech is characterised by strong logic and appropriate means of argumentation.

The scientific style usually demonstrates a great number of references to sources of procedural legislation to the facts:

(29) *Факт хищения Щербининым из квартиры Алимпиевой Л.Н. полностью подтверждается следующими* ***доказательствами: / показаниями потерпевшего Струкова, / оглашенными показаниями потерпевшей Алимпиевой, / протоколом опознания Струковым Щербинина, / протоколом изъятия вещей у Щербинина, / протоколом опознания вещей Струковым, / протоколом осмотра места происшествия.*** [The fact of the theft from L. N. Alimpieva's apartment by Sherbinin is fully supported by the following **evidence: / the testimony of the victim Strukov, / the disclosure of evidence of the injured Alimpieva, / the protocol of Shcherbinin's identification made by Strukov, / the protocol of seizure of the objects from Shcherbinin, / the protocol of identification of the things made by Strukov, / the protocol of inspection of the place of the incident**] (Makhno, 9–15)

In the speeches for the prosecution there are a large number of citations, usual for the scientific style:

(30) ***Обязанность соблюдать законодательство о государственной тайне вытекает из общеправовой обязанности органов государственной власти, местного самоуправления, должностных лиц, граждан и их объединений соблюдать Конституцию Российской Федерации и законы*** *(статья 15, часть 2 Конституции РФ).* [**The obligation to comply with the state secrecy laws is derived from the common law duty of public authorities, local self-government, officials, citizens and their associations to observe the Constitution and the laws of the Russian Federation** (Article 15, Part 2 of the Constitution of the Russian Federation)] (Kondakov, 21)

(31) *Согласно заключению судебно-медицинского эксперта,* ***"Козыревой были причинены: три ушибленные раны правой лобной области и правой теменной области головы; переломы костей свода и основания черепа;***

ушиб вещества головного мозга; одиннадцать проникающих колото-резаных ранений груди с повреждением левого легкого." [According to the medical examiner, "**Kozyreva suffered: three contused wounds of the right frontal region of the head and of the right parietal region of the head, fractures of the calvarium and the skull base; contusion of the brain substance; eleven penetrating stab wounds to the chest with the injury of the left lung**"] (Abramov 2002, 212)

(32) As the judgment emphasised | "**this passage gives too little weight to the dangers of convicting on uncorroborated evidence of identity**" (Andrade, 62–63)

(33) He said | "**Give me all the money**…" (Whylie, 34–35)

A trial speech is a purposeful volitional act in which a prosecutor proves the existence of a crime (Antonenko 1999, 136), so the frequent use of links to sources for specific facts and to opinions of competent people are characteristics of the scientific style.

Some researchers also mention the bright conversational traits of modern judicial speeches (Makarova 1985, 9), but, in my opinion, more likely one can speak only about the elements of the colloquial style in public prosecutor speech, as the goal of the colloquial style is to exchange thoughts, impressions and communication. This goal does not match the purpose of persuasion characteristic for a public speech at the court. Normative judicial speech is devoid of vulgar and everyday words and unnecessary neologisms. A lawyer's speech must be ethically restrained, and the difficulties and misfortunes of people must not get worse due to vulgar public mockery (Enikeev 1996, 274). However, in prosecution speech we can observe lexemes which are characteristic of the colloquial style: emotionally coloured words, words with a figurative sense, parenthetical words, and repetition of words. For example:

Emotionally coloured words:

(34) ***гнусные*** *преступления,* ***великий*** *советский народ,* ***злейшие*** *враги* [**filthy** crimes, the **great** Soviet people, the **bitter** enemies] (Pokrovskiy 2, 6, 12)

Words with a figurative meaning:

(35) ***Первую скрипку играли*** *белоэмигранты* ... / ***Факты оживают*** / *и начинают* ***говорить*** [**The first violin was played** by the White-Guard émigrés (the ones who left Russia with the White Guard in early Soviet period) ... / **The facts are coming to life** / and are starting **to speak**] (Vyshinskiy, 257, 518–519)

Parenthetical words:

(36) ***Конечно***... [**Sure** ...] (Melnikov, 215)
(37) ...***наверное***... [... **maybe** ...] (Salnikov, 62)
(38) **Apparently**... (Whylie, 196)
(39) **Perhaps** ... (Tepleman, 53)

Repetition of words:

(40) *Скоро исполнится* ***три года***_..., ***три года*** ... [Soon it will be **three years** ..., **three years** ...] (Krylenko, 2–3)
(41) *Религиозность* ***русского*** *крестьянина,* ***русского*** *рабочего,* ***русского*** *обывателя* ... ***с целью*** *классовой,* ***с целью*** *ниспровержения* ... [The religiosity of the **Russian** peasant, the **Russian** worker, the **Russian** man in the street ... **with the aim of** the class, **with the aim of** overthrowing the ...] (Krassikov, 38)

Thus, some elements of the colloquial style penetrate into the genre of the speech for the prosecution.

Having examined the functioning of the speech genre of prosecution speech, we can conclude that it contains features of the publicistic, official, scientific and colloquial styles. However, the peculiarities of these styles are unevenly distributed in the speeches of public prosecutors: the signs of the publicistic style dominate in prosecution speeches before a trial by jury in the nineteenth and twenty-first centuries in Russia, in English-speaking prosecutors before a trial by jury at the beginning of the twenty-first century, and in Russian-speaking prosecutors before a professional trial in the 1920s to 1940s. Signs of the official style dominate in speeches of Russian-speaking prosecutors before a professional trial at the beginning of the twenty-first century.

We have studied the characteristics of prosecution speeches as a special speech genre. Now let us turn to the issues related to research methods of studying the speech behaviour of public prosecutors in this speech genre from the point of view of pragmalinguistics.

2. Individual speech behaviour of prosecutors from the point of view of pragmalinguistics

Speech behaviour is considered an automatic stereotypical speech manifestation, without conscious motivation, due to typical repeated situations of speech (Formanovskaya 1989, 28), and individual speech manifestation. We must distinguish "speech behaviour" and "speech activity," because speech activity is motivated and dependent on target speech manifestation (Matveeva 1998, 14).

Speech activity of public prosecutors in the speeches for the prosecution was thoroughly examined by scientists from the point of view of rhetoric (Alexandrov 1993; Apresyan 1969; Arotser 1999; Baev 2000; Baskov 1968, 1986; Danilevich 1991; Ekzempliarov 1976; Golev 1999; Ivakina 2000; Ivin 2002; Kokhtev 1994; Kravchenko, n.d.; Likas 1971, 1990; Melnik 2000; Mikhailovskaya 1981; Panicheva, n.d.; Podgolin 1981; Porubov 2001; Rokhlin, Dvorianskiy 1994; Savitskiy 1971; Tornaev 1999; Tsariov 1983; Volkodaev 1980; Volkov 2001; Vvedenskaya 1994; Zagorskiy 1998; Zaychik 1970; Zubarev 1996) and were given general recommendations for delivering speeches in a trial.

We are analysing speech behaviour of public prosecutors from the standpoint of pragmalinguistic analysis, which studies the impact of an author of a text on their listener. Any form of verbal communication, especially oral, presupposes influence upon an addressee. Moreover, even a neutral joint presence has an impact of one person on another. Problems of communication and impact have been studied by many scholars: Adcock 1964; Ageeva 1989; Bach, n.d.; Belyaeva 1985; Boyko 1989; Butussova 2003; Charleston 1960; Chernoivanova 1998; Chigridova 2001; Chigridova, Kholodkova 2001; Egorshina 1997; Faydysh 1989; Foss, Hakes 1978; Gamble 1990; Gofman 1971; Gorlo 2004; Khanin 1989; Kochkin, n.d.; Kovaliov 1989; Leech 1985; Lenets 1999, 2001; Leontiev 1969, 1999; Lye, n.d.; Mac Cann 1988; Mackenzie 1979; Matveeva 1984, 1985, 1986, 1990, 1993; Mkrtchyan 2004; Moiseenko 2000; Sheinov 2001; Tannen, n.d.; Tarassov 1990; Vassilyeva 1985; Vinokur 1993.

For a successful impact on a listener, a public prosecutor should act according to the well-known Cooperative principle or the Conversational maxims, put forward by Grice (1975). The Cooperative principle means that any contribution to a speech exchange is engaged in as required by the accepted purpose or direction of the speech. The Cooperative principle includes four maxims:

The maxim of Quality

Try to make your contribution one that is true, specifically:
(1) do not say what you believe to be false,
(2) do not say that for which you lack adequate evidence.

The maxim of Quantity

(1) make your contribution as informative as is required for the current purpose of the exchange,
(2) do not make your contribution more informative than is required.

The maxim of Relevance

Make your contributions relevant.

The maxim of Manner

Be perspicuous, and specifically:
(1) avoid obscurity,
(2) avoid ambiguity,
(3) be brief,
(4) be orderly (Grice, 1975).

Let us now analyse the four maxims.

The maxim of Quality

The statement must be true. Do not say what you think is false, or what you cannot prove. In accordance with the law, a public prosecutor must support the prosecution only if they are firmly convinced of the defendant's guilt, if the examined evidence is supportive enough for it. In modern Russia, if a prosecutor comes to the opposite conclusion, their duty is to repudiate the charges.

The maxim of Quantity

The statement is to contain no less and no more information than is required to meet current aims of the dialogue. Awareness of the speaker must exceed the awareness of the listeners. The speech will be effective only when there is some kind of "difference of potentials" between the speaker's knowledge and the audience's awareness (Nozhin 1973, 46). It is believed that the speaker is able to keep the audience in a state of tension if they know that they have information which is three or four times more than that of the listeners (Andreev 1993, 133). However, it does not mean that a public prosecutor should be verbose. Do not talk too much. Verbiage can only weaken the attention to the incontrovertible evidence.

The maxim of Relevance

A public prosecutor should not deviate from the main subject of the message. The court in Russia cannot restrict the duration of the public prosecutor's speech at regular intervals, but the judge has a right to stop them if they deal with circumstances unrelated to the case.

Moreover, not only from the legal but also from the psychological point of view, a public prosecutor should not talk too much in their speech. The knowledge that an addresser is given to say useless things reduces the audience's attention, and a public prosecutor should give some rest for the attention of judges (especially the jury) not by giving pointless arguments, but by repeating the essential arguments of the prosecution (Sergeich 1988, 30). A public prosecutor always has something important to say and he should not waste valuable time.

The maxim of Manner

Speak clearly and avoid ambiguous phrases, or in other words be short and organised. A listener does not want to be involved in difficulty of word choice. Smoothness, lightness and elegance of speech give pleasure precisely because it does not require a great deal of effort for perception (Massarskiy 1979, 38–39). At the trial, there should not just be clear speech but extraordinary clarity. Listeners must understand without effort. The speaker can rely on their imagination, but not on their mind and insight. Having understood, they will go further but if it does not happen they will reach a deadlock (Sergeich 1988, 18). This is due to the fact that a public prosecutor creates a simple picture of the world for listeners. Only in exchange for clarity can a person take another's point of view concerning life. It is possible to convince only by showing that the addressee's clarity is deceptive, that they do not see one or the other, that the picture is much more complicated than it seems to a listener. In all cases, a speaker counts not on concealing the truth, but rather on clarifying the situation (Khazagerov, n.d.).

Thus, a public prosecutor, for a successful impact on the listener, must follow the Cooperative principle, including the maxims of Quality, Quantity, Relevance and Manner.

The issues of speech influence and the relationships of linguistic signs and people who create, accept and understand these signs are in the field of pragmalinguistics. Pragmalinguistics, as an aspect of semiotics, involves a complex of issues associated with a speaking subject, an addressee, and their interaction in communication, in a communication situation (Arutyunova 2000, 390).

A peculiar feature of judicial speech is the presence of some speakers: the judges, the adversary, the defendant and the public. Prosecutor speeches are primarily addressed to the judges, without doubt the main addressee. Each speech begins with an appeal to the judges or, of course, to the jury. Another addressee of a judicial speech is the speaker's adversary whose argument, evidence or conclusion must be disputed. Due to the criminal procedure in modern Russia, a state prosecutor cannot directly address those present in the courtroom, but nevertheless they implicitly address both the defendant to correct them and the audience to prevent a crime. In pre-revolutionary Russia a prosecutor could directly address the defendant:

> *Что еще говорили вы? Что капитал был вам подарен двумя лицами?* [*What else did you say? That the capital had been given to you by two men?*] (Kazarinov, 152–153).

Therefore, a judicial speech is characterised by the presence of not one but four addressees: the judges, the adversary, the defendant and the public. To the last two addressees, a state prosecutor addresses implicitly. Successful cooperation between an addresser and an addressee is associated with what is considered to be the subject of pragmalinguistics.

The subject of pragmalinguistics is the issue connected to the choice of language means from an available repertoire for the best impact (Stepanov 1981, 325), the problem being one of choice of those units from a number of synonyms with the help of which the speaker has the maximum impact on the addressee. In addition, this choice has the least conscious character of the least deliberate action (Saussure 1990, 41).

Implicit pragmalinguistics studies the selection of signals of grammatical categories made by communicants automatically. As this choice is familiar, it was made a lot of times, and such a choice is called "speech behaviour." We also study stereotyped speech behaviour of public prosecutors in a court statement, and in the next section will consider the peculiarities of stereotyped speech behaviour in the speech genre of prosecution speech.

3. Stereotyped speech behaviour of prosecutors from the point of view of pragmalinguistics

Homo sapiens is the only kind on earth to not have a strictly determined, genetic program of life activity. Unlike a human being, other animals have a model of fixed actions which can include a complex sequence of performance (rituals of courtship, coupling, etc.). The fundamental feature characteristic for these models is a consistent repetition of reactions while being presented certain stimuli. With regard to a human being, scientists have come to the conclusion that the genetic background determines about 50 percent of personal characteristics, and 50 percent of these characteristics are influenced by the external environment (Rowe 1989).

Not having a program of life, the only way for a human being to survive is to rely on the social reality, which is a specific natural area, created by people themselves. With the help of the process of socialisation, as well as with the help of a permanent process of getting and using information, a human being acts according to certain patterns of behaviour. Thus, a person acquires a program of life, which is, by its nature, externally determined (Chuldini, n.d.).

It causes, on the one hand, freedom of choice and a wide field for human creativity and self-realisation, while on the other it causes flexibility and mobility of the program of activity. Psyche and perception of a person are also mobile systems. However, the extreme mobility of the human world would threaten his existence. Therefore, they try their best to maintain stable behaviour, follow the rules and norms accepted in society through the repetition of certain stereotypical reactions to socially important stimuli. The stability of behaviour is maintained by social reflexes developed in the course of the evolution through ready-made models of behaviour.

The cause of stereotyping and simplification of thought and behaviour of a person is the inability to analyse every aspect of a diverse, multi-dimensional social reality. Sometimes life questions are too complex, there is limited time to spare, or emotional excitement is too strong and so a person has to respond stereotypically and immediately, without any prior analysis of the information, or, we can say, at the unconscious level. The expression of this level is in the typical individual's unconsciousness of those structural features, boundaries, and significant elements of behaviour which are always used by a person implicitly (Sapir 1993, 598).

The implicit following of some definite stereotypes of behaviour depends on the belonging of an addresser to a particular social group, to some significant terms and circumstances of communication (Makarov 1998, 68–75; Karassik 2000, 37–64). These circumstances may include: (a) communicative intentions of an author; (b) relationships between an addresser and addressees; (c) all sorts of "facts" that are meaningful and random; (d) common ideological features and the stylistic climate of the era in general, and of particular environment and specific individuals to whom the information is directly or indirectly addressed, in particular; (e) genre and stylistic features of both the message and the communicative situation in which it is included; and (f) the set of associations with the previous experience (Gasparov 1996, 10)

That is why not every person is able to explain why they act in particular situations in different ways. It is due to the human psyche. Psyche is a function of the brain, and is a function of one part of the organism, the side through which all the variety of effects on the body of the external world, and especially social reality, is carried out. The influence of the outside world—individual social experience—creates complex dynamic system functional formations of the brain, that humans, from the social and psychological point of view, consider to be the concept of personality (Myasishchev 1960, 10).

The formation of individual culture of a member of society is determined by social consciousness. Consciousness has three main levels—existential, reflexive and spiritual (Zinchenko 1997). It is the existential level of consciousness which is manifested in human communication and behaviour, and this level can be observed. According to the recent data, unconsciousness determines 92–98 percent of human behaviour. The existential level of consciousness is the base, absorbed in childhood and then followed unconsciously. Reflexive consciousness is formed during life through learning, teaching, knowledge transferring, meditations on reality, on behaviour of others and one's own behaviour. The spiritual level of consciousness is achieved in society by only a few persons (Sternin, n.d.).

The point is that an individual and society as a whole can have a certain level of reflexive consciousness, learn some of the values at the level of reflection, debate them, declare and welcome them, but also keep old existential consciousness and previous behaviour, including, of course, former speech behaviour.

From an early age, a child copies the behaviour of the adults around them. However, a simple copy is not yet a stereotype. A certain fact of behaviour becomes a stereotype of behaviour only when it is observed often, repeated, and as a consequence of this multiple repetition is carried to automatism.

Stereotyped speech behaviour can be due to the constant social characteristics of a person: their social position, profession, age, sex and marital status; and due to variable characteristics determined by the situation: the role of a buyer, a passenger, a client (Kryssin 1976, 43). Therefore, a person's belonging to a particular professional type requires them to have an idea of the typical stereotypes of professional conduct (Petrenko 1988, 102).

The profession of communicants affects people's perception of each other. Especially after being in long-term professional activity, humans form stereotyped behaviour, usually called a "professional habit." This habit is most pronounced in the professional activity of doctors, actors, writers, law enforcement officials—all of those in whose daily work another person is the central figure (Bodaliov 1995, 168). Undoubtedly, this fact also applies to public prosecutors, and it is not by accident that there is such a expression in the Russian language as a "prosecutor's tone."

In the nature of the reactions of every person, in the peculiarities of behaviour and speech, there are variants. When these variants of reaction transfer from casual to permanent, but are still not formed into pathology, one can tell identify accentuations of personal traits. Approximately one half of the population is considered to be accentuated personalities, and the other half is not as conspicuous (Leongard 1981, 271). Accentuations of a character are extreme variants of a norm where certain traits of character are greatly predominant (Pushkina 1996, 34).

A character trait is a significant attitude to the facts of life and to one's own actions. Adherence to principles, cheerfulness, honesty, exactingness, rigor, sensitivity, sociability and other traits of character are definite, rooted in relationships to reality, society, labour, and to others and oneself (Lichko 1983, 22).

Speaking of accentuated personalities, it would also be reasonable to talk about professional accentuations, that is, typical features which are crucial for a person of any profession. A professional accentuation is a combination of mental and psycho-physiological traits of human personality, expressed in peculiarities of appearance, habits of dressing, behaviour, and specific features of mind and speech which exist in the form of inclinations or which are formed under the influence of a profession (Lomova 2004, 43).

The professional activity of a public prosecutor has a significant impact on their personality, affecting their psychological characteristics, as well as manner of communication. The public nature of their activity, the powers of authority and a high level of responsibility often lead a public prosecutor to professional "deformation."

The term "deformation" is used to refer to various changes in the shape of objects and phenomena of the external world, including personality changes which happen under the influence of a profession, and the activity of a public prosecutor is not an exception in this respect.

Deformations of the individuality of a public prosecutor do not happen spontaneously, because of aging, but as a result of the activities they carry out. For example, it was found that professionally important characteristics of cognitive processes tend to be improved or stabilised, depending on the length of working, and the parameters that do not participate in professional activities deteriorate. At the same time, there is a reduction and stereotyping of ranges, of kinds of professional activities, of which the most effective behavioural reactions remain. Among personal features, the changes are reflected in the growth of self-esteem. According to received information, the degree of extra-high self-esteem is in direct proportion to the length of service, and at the same time there is also the rise of professional identity (Rogov 1994, 208).

The legal profession of a public prosecutor promotes both positive qualities (high moral principles, endurance, calmness, discipline, open-mindedness and the ability to communicate to people and to establish contact with them) and negative ones (indifference to people, their lives, feelings and interests, excessive suspicion, rudeness, careerism, etc.).

One of the most dangerous types of professional deformation of a public prosecutor is being too suspicious. They often lose faith in people, willing to suspect everyone. In any omission they see an evil intent, in each suspect a criminal. Gradually, such an attitude leads to the formation of a pronounced pessimism and intolerance with respect to people. From the psychological point of view, evaluation expresses the qualities of not only those who are the subjects of the estimation, but also the personality of the judging. In these evaluations and experiences it is seen the level of development of a person as a representative of a certain class or group as a member of a particular team. These evaluations show civil and psychological maturity, some features of a profession, and moral and aesthetic requirements for people. Nevertheless, they always have the unique stamp of a person who was formed as a very specific personality (Myasishchev 1970, 115), and this is confirmed in speech. The specificity of communication, unlike any other type of interaction, is in the fact that it reveals the psychological qualities of people.

All things considered, one must say that speech behaviour and personal characteristics of communicators represent the inseparable unity of individual, social and national-cultural peculiarities of behaviour. However, we believe that the specificity of expression and combination of these features varies depending on the specific situations of communication, including speech genres. It is reasonable now to turn to the methods of studying speech behaviour of public prosecutors in Implicit Pragmalinguistics.

4. Methods of studying the speech behaviour of public prosecutors in Implicit Pragmalinguistics

Within the bounds of Implicit Pragmalinguistics there are such methods of investigation as:

- synchronous personal (when we study the texts of different genres created by the same author in the same period of time),
- diachronic personal (when we study the texts of one author, of one genre, but created in different age periods),
- synchronous interpersonal (when we study the texts of the same speech genre created by different authors in the same period time) (Matveeva 2001, 51–52).

The present study uses the “synchronous personal” method when analysing the speech behaviour of one public prosecutor, Truhanov Gennadiy Vladimirovich, in different speech genres (in a speech before a trial by jury, in a speech before a professional trial and in his article from the newspaper *Vecherniy Rostov* [*Evening Rostov*]), and the “synchronous interpersonal” method in studying the speeches for the prosecution of different prosecutors in the same period of time (the end of the nineteenth century in Russia, the 1920s to 1940s in the USSR, and the beginning of the twenty-first century in Russia and Great Britain).

The kinds of speech behaviour are called “implicit strategies of the addresser’s speech influence on the addressee.” These strategies can be divided into two groups: emotion-oriented and connotative-oriented (Matveeva 1993, 96–262).

Emotion-oriented strategies, as well as the emotive function of speech, are focused on the addresser of the text (in our case, on a public prosecutor), who express their subjective, psychological attitude to what they is saying. The emotive function is associated with the subjective world of the addresser, with the expression of their feelings, their attitude to what is said, and this function reflects the speaker's self-esteem, and their need to be heard and understood (Kunitsyna 2002, 61). There are different kinds of emotion-oriented strategies:

- "Participation/Nonparticipation of members of communication in a speech event"
- "Sure/Unsure speech behaviour of an author"
- "The author's probabilistic evaluation of a speech event as real / unreal."

Connotative-oriented strategies reflect a speech behaviour of a prosecutor directed at the receiver. The title of this strategy contains a reference to another function of speech—connotative (regulatory or directive). The connotative function reflects certain needs of a person, for example, to achieve goals or to influence other people (Kunitsyna 2002, 61), and here follows a list of connotative-oriented strategies:

- "The sender's formation of addressee's attitude to a speech event by evaluation"
- "The author's accentuating of the elements of an utterance"
- "Satisfaction / dissatisfaction of addressee's pragmatic expectations by an addresser" (Matveeva 1998, 44–45).

In our study, within the bounds of the pragmalinguistic experiment, we analyse the speech behaviour of the public prosecutors in accordance with the emotion-oriented strategies "Participation/nonparticipation of members of communication in a speech event" and "Sure/Unsure speech behaviour of an author," and according to the connotative-oriented strategy "The sender's formation of addressee's attitude to a speech event by evaluation."

To begin, we will give an example of analysis of the public prosecutor's speech behaviour with the help of a synchronous personal approach to the texts of various genres created in one period (January to June 2003), by the author Trukhanov, who is also a public prosecutor of the Regional Prosecutor's Office (Rostov-on-Don, Russia). We will try to answer the following questions:

- Are the speech behaviours of the prosecutor in speeches before a professional trial, before the jury and in the article on criminal law for the newspaper the same or different?
- If these speech behaviours are different, what is the reason for these discrepancies?

We analysed 1,214 minor syntactic groups (MSG) according to the enumerated strategies as recorded in table 1 (see appendix). Let us study the actualisation of the implicit speech strategies in more detail.

I. "Participation/Nonparticipation of members of communication in a speech event"

This strategy is actualised in one of the three following speech planes: the plane of personal participation, the plane of social participation, and the plane of objective participation (Matveeva 1993, 98–101). Using the "personal plane," the author actualises the participation either of an addresser or an addressee in a speech event. "Social plane" shows us that both an addresser and an addressee act in communication. Finally, in the plane of objective participation the addressee's attention focuses on the objectivity of a speech event, regardless of participation/nonparticipation of the members of communication.

According to the results of the studied texts, the average speech-genre index of the plane of objective participation is the highest at 76.2 percent. It is interesting to note that the index of the plane of objective participation in the speech before a professional court (92. 6 percent) is nearly equal to the same index of the newspaper article (92.5 percent). The predominance of the plane of objective participation in comparison with the other planes of this implicit speech strategy is due to the fact that, on the one hand, the public prosecutor in court must charge the defendant on behalf of the state, to be based only on the factual circumstances of the crime committed by the defendant. A prosecutor has no right to evaluate the evidence publicly, or to give any comments. For this purpose, a public prosecutor has no appropriate procedural forms. On the other hand, the high index of the plane of objective participation in the newspaper article relates to the fact that the main task of the author is to inform readers about the situation in the Regional Court of Rostov-on-Don as impartially as it is possible. In both cases, the focus on the objective sides of reality arouses the readers' trust in the given facts.

The average speech-genre index of the plane of personal participation is 16.2 percent. The highest index of this plane (22.7 percent) can be seen in the speech of Trukhanov before the jurors. The author is unconsciously eager to be the leader, and influences the jurors with the power of his authority. Whereas in the speech for the newspaper article the state prosecutor intuitively does not aim to have a personal impact on the readers, and here the index of the plane of personal participation is just 5.9 percent. There is also a relatively low level of the plane of personal participation in Trukhanov's speech before professional judges (7.4 percent), as the state prosecutor speaks not before a heterogeneous audience, as is the case with a trial by the jury, but the people of the same profession, of the same level of education, who are already specialists in the details of the case. The speeches to the professional judges are very formal, and are always prepared according to a well-known pattern. Here, the state prosecutor unconsciously tries to influence the professional trial not by the force of his authority, but by giving the information about the facts of the case.

With regard to the actualisation of the plane of social participation, it can be correlated with the cooperative type of behaviour. The division into "we" and "they" is more ancient than the division into "I" and "you." "We" is considered to be someone's own, to be close; whereas, "they" is considered to be somebody else's, to be strange. The internal doubts of a person, their hesitations while making every decision, is the process of experience and the choice of the answers to the following questions: Who is the closest? Who is a friend? Who is a stranger or even an enemy? To persuade, a public prosecutor must attract the positive attitude of their audience. That is why the highest level of the "social plane" (12 percent) is in Trukhanov's speech before the jury. The public prosecutor is trying to become as close to the jury as it is possible. As psychologists say, representatives of the jury are guided by their own reason, conscience, life experience, sense of justice and duty, and responsibility (Chufarovskiy 1995, 233). Therefore, creating a sense of community and personal trust between a public prosecutor and a diverse group of jurors cannot be overestimated.

To a lesser degree, the plane of social participation is actualised by Trukhanov when speaking to the reader of the newspaper (1.6 percent). In addition, we do not see signs of this plane in the speech before the professional judges. To my mind, here the author does not seek cooperation, as he understands that the powers of the prosecutor and the judges are clearly differentiated, and often the judge already has his own point of view which is why the speech of the public prosecutor is formal in this case. Such trials differ from trials by the jury, which demand the adversarial principle, requiring the public prosecutor to demonstrate high professionalism and personal responsibility.

As we can see, the variants of speech behaviour of the public prosecutor in accordance with the implicit speech strategy "Participation / nonparticipation of members of communication in a speech event" are different when considering the text, and each time they solve different problems, serve specific goals and objectives of the sender of the messages constructed by the unwritten laws of the particular speech genre of the particular situation and addressee. At the same time, the skill to adapt his speech to different concrete conditions of speech when creating the texts of specific speech genres testifies to the speech skills of Trukhanov, and his not so young age (he is 40 years old), which has helped him to gain professional experience.

II. "Sure/Unsure speech behaviour of an author"

This strategy is actualised with the help of two speech planes: the first is certain statement and the second one is uncertain statement.

The prosecutor in court has complete autonomy in determining the line of his conduct and decision making. Law and materials of the case are the main determinants for the actions of the prosecutor in court. He is not bound by the conclusions of the indictment, even by his own. If the accusation made by investigative agencies finds no evidence in court, the prosecutor has the right to refuse it (Alekseev 1998, 102).

The belief in personal rightness is the main quality of a public prosecutor. To have an impact on another person, especially on a group of individuals that differ by sex, age, temperament, education, intelligence level etc., a public prosecutor must possess a certain amount of personal socio-psychological characteristics. These qualities include a high level of initiative, organisational skills and experience, interest in achieving goals, being well informed, sociable and personally appealing, and, finally, a high level of their own prestige and authority (Porubov 2001, 76).

In short, the behaviour of a public prosecutor must be confident, and the same quality should extend to their speech as a representative of the law. The materials of our study support this position. The average speech-genre index of the certain statement in Trukhanov's speeches is relatively frequent (39.5 percent).

The highest index of the certain statement is in the court speech for the jurors (48.8 percent) where the task of persuasion is extremely important. In legal psychology, it is known that it is possible to persuade or convince the addressee only if a speaker is firmly convinced in their own rightness.

It lends passion, emotion and power to the speeches, A confident speaker makes the jury believe them by sharing emotions and sincerity, and can more easily influence their minds, convince them of the correctness of their views, and persuade them to make the necessary decisions (Shikhantsov 1998, 301).

However, the speech before the professional judges of the public prosecutor Trukhanov differs from the others through examples of caution, according to the highest index of uncertain statement (77.4 percent). In this case, the public prosecutor is intuitively less categorical which helps him to avoid antagonism from the same professionals as he is.

Therefore, in the implicit speech strategy "Sure/Unsure speech behaviour of an author," the indices of the planes of certain/uncertain statement are also different, as in the previous strategy, and depend on the addressees of the information.

III. "The sender's formation of addressee's attitude to a speech event by evaluation"

In any message there are two sides: rational and emotional. The rational acts with the help of evidence, specific facts, and the force of logic; the emotional does its job with the help of listener's senses, caused at the moment of transferring the message. The way to a human heart is not only through the mind but also the emotions (Porubov 2001, 81).

Even in the nineteenth century it was known that the jury does not argue about what crime the defendant committed but about what kind of a person they are (Sergeich 2000, 127). That is, the emotional side of things and evaluation of the deeds play an important role in reaching a verdict.

There are three planes of the implicit speech strategy "the sender's formation of addressee's attitude to a speech event by evaluation." They are: the plane of positive attitude, the plane of neutral attitude and the plane of negative attitude.

The general aim of the prosecutor's speech is forming a negative attitude to a crime, a consequence of the functions of the speeches for the prosecution. The average speech-genre index of the plane of forming negative attitude towards a speech event in the studied texts is 38.6 percent. The highest "negative" index is in Trukhanov's speech before the professional judges, at 49.1 percent, whereas he has the lowest index of forming positive attitude, only 3.5 percent. Most likely this is due to the widespread characteristic of the courts without a jury to convict. It will be enough to say that in Russia 18 percent of verdicts are "not guilty" in trials by jury, and only 0.02 percent in an ordinary court, that is a professional one.

The lowest index of neutral evaluation (43.5 percent) is in the newspaper article, whereas the average speech-genre index is 52.7 percent. This is due to the fact that, as a rule, a newspaper text is effecting and expressive. Moreover, also here is the highest positive index (11. 5 percent) and a relatively high negative attitude (45 percent). Therefore, the total emotional intensity is 56.5 percent. In this article, the author is eager to attract the readers' interest to the information, often unconsciously actualising both positive and negative kinds of evaluation of the events.

In accordance with the studied strategy, we can conclude that the author actualises negative, positive and neutral kinds of evaluation, depending on what kind of attitude to the information provided the prosecutor wants an addressee to have.

The study shows that the speech behaviour of an individual is not an invariable system and changes depending on the situation of interaction, without losing its specificity. After analysing the speech of the public prosecutor in the synchronous personal approach in the aspect of implicit pragmalinguistics, we can now answer the questions posed earlier.

The variants of speech behaviour of the public prosecutor Truhanov in the different texts (the speech before a trial by jury, before a professional trial and the article from the newspaper *Vecherniy Rostov/Evening Rostov*) have some common features (similar indices of a personal, social and objective planes of the implicit speech strategy "Participation/ nonparticipation of members of communication in a speech event," relatively similar rates of the planes of certain/uncertain statement of the implicit speech strategy "Sure/Unsure speech behaviour of an author" in the speech before professional judges and in the newspaper article; the predominance of negative attitude in all three texts) and significant distinctive features (especially that the indices of all planes are different in the speech before a trial by jury compared to the speaking before professional judges and in the newspaper article). Most likely, it depends on different goals and objectives of the author and on various addressees of these texts.

PART II

INDIVIDUAL SPEECH BEHAVIOUR OF PROSECUTORS OF ENGLISH-SPEAKING AND RUSSIAN-SPEAKING LINGUA-CULTURAL COMMUNITIES IN IMPLICIT PRAGMALINGUISTICS

1. Requirements for the linguistic analysis of prosecutors' individual personal qualities in Implicit Pragmalinguistics

The theory and methodology of the pragmalinguistic analysis were created by Matveeva (1999) and further developed by her followers (Bagdassarian 2004; Varnavskikh 2004; Gorlo 2004; Mkrtchyan 2004; Zyubina 2005; Chunachova 2006 and others). The working hypothesis is in the following: if in a text there are emotive- and conative-oriented speech signals of speech behaviour of an author, it is possible to note them, to identify, to single out, to count and to present them in tables considered to be a pragmalinguistic speech portrait of an author (a sender of information). A speech portrait has the power of making a diagnosis: an interpretation of speech portrait's elements allow an opportunity to correlate them with some individual features of an author (Matveeva 1999, 54).

The investigation is carried out according to this plan:

(1) preparing the list of speech signals of sender's speech behaviour in Russian and English
(2) selection of texts-speeches for the prosecution
(3) preparing the texts for the analysis (dividing them into minor syntactic groups—MSG)
(4) preparing table matrices in order to fill them with marks denoting the presence of a definite speech signal
(5) making the analysis: looking for the speech signals in the text and marking them in the table

(6) counting the frequency of the planes' actualisation, making and interpretation the senders' speech portraits, making a diagnosis of their individual features.

Let us study in detail all points of the plan:

A definite number of speech signals (markers) corresponds to each implicit speech strategy. The following are examples of such speech signals or markers.

The Implicit Speech Strategy "Participation/Nonparticipation of Members of Communication in a Speech Event"

This strategy is actualised in one of the three speech planes:

- the plane of personal participation
- the plane of social participation
- the plane of objective participation.

The plane of personal participation implies participation in a speech event of only a sender of communication or its addressee, and it is underlined that it must be only one person. In addition, this plane requires the following speech signals: exclusive personal pronouns (examples 42, 43), indirect forms of exclusive personal pronouns and respective possessive pronouns (examples 44, 45), nouns in a function of exclusive personal pronouns (examples 46, 47), and addresses (examples 48, 49):

(42) **Я** могу сделать это лишь в самом беглом очерке … [**I** can do it only as a sketch] (Muraviov, 12)
(43) … as **I** said before … (Reid, 92)
(44) …что **мое** обвинение несколько разнится от того сознания … [… That **my** accusation somewhat differs from that consciousness …] (Kessel, 28)
(45) If this has ever happened to **you** … (Whylie, 151)
(46) Перед **государственным обвинением** стоит сложная задача … [Before **the state prosecution**_there is a difficult task …] (Agapov, 4)
(47) … that **the jury** are in the best position (Andrade, 9)
(48) **Уважаемые присяжные заседатели!** [**Dear jurors!**] (Melnikov, 1)
(49) **Ladies and gentlemen!** (Kingston, 1)

In the above examples (42–49), the authors actualise participation in a speech event as either a sender or an addressee of communication.

The markers of the plane of personal participation are also forms of a verb in the passive voice with local and temporal determinations of the type "here" and "now." Moreover, in an MSG a participant is not expressed but one of the participants of a definite speech event is implied so it is clear who this person is:

(50) Действия подсудимых по данному эпизоду **квалифицируются** по ст. 158 ч.3 п. "б" УК РФ [The actions of the defendants in this episode **are classified** under Art. 158, Part 3, subsection "b" of the Criminal Code of the Russian Federation] (Agapov, 22)
(51) All the circumstances **are shown** in this speech (Kingston, 310). Imperative exclusive forms of verbs are also the markers of the plane of personal participation
(52) **Забудьте** хотя бы на некоторое время о своих проблемах и заботах… [At least for some time **forget** about your problems and concerns …] (Trukhanov, 6)
(53) **Think** of that with care … (Dennis, 43)

Here a prosecutor directly addresses to a trial by jury actualising the plane of personal participation of the implicit speech strategy "Participation/ nonparticipation of members of communication in a speech event."

Verbal lexemes of the type "seem," "look," and "appear" corresponding to one of the participants of a real speech event (examples 54–55) and parenthetical words especially modal words and some adverbs denoting attitude (examples 56–57) are markers of the plane of personal participation:

(54)Данное объяснение **представляется** наиболее обоснованным. [This explanation **seems** the most reasonable one] (Melnikov, 202)
(55) He **appears** to be an honest person (Kingston, 22)
(56) **К счастью**… [**Fortunately** …] (Plevako, 519)
(57) Experience has **undoubtedly** shown … (Smith, 115)

In all of these examples, there is a personal attitude of the author in the speech event.

Moreover, the meaning of higher degree of probability may be also expressed with the help of such combinations as "to be sure/to be certain +

Infinitive," and the meaning of supposition with the help of the word combination "to be likely + Infinitive":

(58) And new trials **are certain to** be ordered (Kingston, 399)
(59) Any difference **is likely to** be of significance … (Templeman, 168)

The sender implicitly shows his own participation in the process of uttering.

The markers of **the plane of social participation** are inclusive personal pronouns (examples 60–61), nouns in a function of inclusive personal pronouns (examples 62–63):

(60) … пройти **вместе с Вами** через лабиринт сомнений и неуверенности… [… to go along **with you** through the maze of doubt and uncertainty …] (Trukhanov, 46)
(61) **We** must know… (Kingston, 365)
(62) **Пролетарскому Суду** никогда за все семь с половиной лет революции не приходилось чинить суда над человеком … [During all these seven and a half years of the revolution **the Proletarian Court** had never to put on trial a man …] (Koni, 6)
(63) Even **honest witnesses** can give inaccurate evidence … (Dennis, 52)

Regarding a kind of participation in which both a sender and an addressee take part, we can also judge according to the following markers: a form of a verb in the third person plural with a latent participant (examples 64–65), an infinitive (examples 66–67), indefinite and negative pronouns (examples 68–69), lexemes with a seme of anthroponym such as "nation," "mankind," "people" and others (examples 70–71), impersonal sentences (examples 72–73):

(64) Доказательства **позволяют** воспроизвести истинную картину происшедшего. [The proofs **make** it **possible** to reproduce the true picture of what happened.] (Salnikov, 225)
(65) **Могут возникнуть** два обоснованных вопроса … [Two legitimate questions **may arise** …] (Melnikov, 80)
(66) Наступило время **подвести** итоги, правильно **оценить** доказательства и **сделать** выводы. [It is time to take stock, to properly assess the evidence and draw conclusions.] (Fiodorov, 3–5)

(67) This is a question **to be considered** in the round … (Templeman, 16)
(68) Это ясно **любому**. [It is clear to **any** person.] (Trukhanov, 474)
(69) **No one** knows (Reid, 121)
(70) Еще на заре цивилизации **человечество** выработало заповедь … [Even at the dawn of civilization **the mankind** had a Commandment …] (Abramov, 2)
(71) **English people** have no doubt … (Kingston, 113)
(72) **Как видно… [It can be seen** …] (Abramov, 248)
(73) Now **it is clear** … (Whylie, 158).

To the plane of social participation we refer a passive form of a verb with a latent participant. In such a case, this latent participant can be both a sender and an addressee, with a condition that this participant is not clear from the context but we can guess the definite participant on the assumption of the situation (Матвеева 1993, 155–156). More often, it is a passive form of a verb with a modal verb:

(74) В судебном заседании **исследовались** также протоколы осмотра ножа и топора … [At the court session the reports of inspection of the knife and the hatchet **were** also **examined** …] (Kozyr, 72)
(75) The material facts of this case **can be** shortly **summarised** as follows (Reid, 1)

Imperative inclusive forms of a verb (examples 76–77) and adjectives with suffixes -able, -ible (example 78) are also signals of the plane of social participation:

(76) **Давайте** еще раз вместе **проанализируем** доказательства по данному делу. [**Let's analyse** the evidence of the case once again] (Kozyr, 47)
(77) … **see** the report of the decision of the Court of Appeal in 1978 … (Whylie, 189)
(78) The visual identification is **unreliable** (Smith, 277)

The list of the markers of **the plane of objective participation** includes the rest of the markers which are not used for the plane of personal participation and the plane of social participation. For example, here one can see speech signals referring to a actor that is not a participant of this speech event (neither a sender nor an addressee) (examples 79–80), a passive form which indicates a person or an object, or we can guess what they are, but which do not take part in a speech event (examples 81–82):

(79) **Эта социальная группа** отжила свой век… [**This social group** outlived its time …] (Krylenko, 766)
(80) **Patricia Elvin** heard an explosion … (Dennis, 5)
(81) Гражданин Будков **задержан** за особо тяжкое преступление… [Budkov **is arrested** for a very serious crime …] (Trukhanov, 14)
(82) On July 2, 1981 the appellant **was arrested** for murder (Dennis, 20)

Neither sender's nor addressee's participations are actualised in these speech events. The authors draw our attention to the objective character of the processes in these speech events, and one should notice that it happens without any participation of senders and addressees.

We have examined the speech signals actualising in a speech act of an English-speaking and a Russian-speaking prosecutor on the planes of personal, social and objective participations of the implicit speech strategy "Participation/Nonparticipation of members of communication in a speech event." Now, let us study the signals of the next implicit speech strategy, "Sure/Unsure speech behaviour of an author."

The implicit speech strategy "Sure/Unsure speech behaviour of an author"

This strategy is actualised with the help of two speech planes: the first is certain statement and the second is uncertain statement of an author. For the actualisation of certain statement in the Russian language, one can distinguish the following speech signals: the combination of definite verbal categories—the present tense, active voice, imperfective aspect (example 83); omitted form of the verb "to be" (example 84); indication of the actor in the passive voice (example 85); the combination in a verb of the categories of the future tense and perfective aspect (example 86); inclusion in lexical actualisators the meaning of "demand," "persistence," and "insistence" (example 87); a decisive and repeated negation (example 88); semes indicating the superlative degree or testifying to a "peculiarity" of something (example 89); indicators of a great amount, integrity, adherence to one's principles, globalisation and profoundness (example

90); analytical and semantic intensifiers (example 91); recommendations and appeals (example 92); and addresses (example 93).

(83) Убийство не только **обрывает** жизнь, но и **приносит** глубокую скорбь для родных и близких погибшего. [A murder does not only **take** someone's life, but it also **brings** deep sorrow for the nearest and dearest of a murdered person.] (Abramov, 8–9)

(84) Форма эта—террор, пути—политические убийства, а средство—динамит и целая система взрывов и взрывчатых приспособлений. [This form (is) terror, the ways (are) political assassinations, and the means (are) dynamite and the whole system of explosions and explosive devices.] (Muraviov, 135–137)

(85) … в которых они **обвиняются следствием** … [… in which they **are accused by the judicial investigation** …] (Romanov, 5)

(86) При назначении наказания председательствующий в любом случае **учтет** их несовершеннолетний возраст как смягчающее обстоятельство. [In giving the judgement, in any case the presiding judge **will take into account** their being under age as a mitigating circumstance.] (Salnikov, 359)

(87) Я на этом **настаиваю** … [I **insist** on it …] (Pokrovskiy, 279)

(88) Этот интеллигент **не** верил в революцию, **не** верил партии, **не** верил в нашу власть. [This intellectual **did not** believe in the revolution, **did not** believe the party, **did not** believe our power.] (Kondrushkin, 156–158)

(89) **Конкретнейший** из **конкретнейших** вопросов о "мужике" и был именно вопрос о том … [**The most specific of the most specific** issues about a "peasant" was the very question about …] (Vyshinskiy, 552)

(90) Настоящий процесс дал **огромный** материал … [This process gave a **great** material …] (Lunacharskiy, 1)

(91) **Совершенно** очевидно … [**Absolutely** clearly …] (Pokrovskiy, 22)

(92) … всех обвиняемых по этому делу **расстрелять**! [… **shoot** all the accused!] (Pokrovskiy, 95)

(93) **Милостивые государи** … [**Dear Sirs** …] (Muraviov, 194)

In the English language, certain statement is actualised with the help of the present simple tense (example 94), the future simple tense (example 95), infinitive (+ present / future) (examples 96–97), participle I (+ present / future) (example 98), participle II (+ present/future) (examples 99–100), present passive (example 101), modal verbs "must" (example 102), "to have to" (example 103), "to be to" (example 104), "should/ought to" (examples 105–106), imperative (example 107), parenthetical word denoting confidence (examples 108–109), not using the sequence of tenses (examples 110–111), emphatic "do" (examples 112–113):

(94) Their Lordships **do not agree** with this appreciation of the law (Tepleman, 1)
(95) Their Lordships **will** first **give** their reasons for their decision … (Smith, 3)
(96) This is a question [**to be considered** in the round] … (Tepleman, 17)
(97) They will say [**to keep** your mouth] (Kingston, 55)
(98) **Signing** it | he will confirm its accuracy (Kingston, 199)
(99) The situation [**created** by the delay] *is* such … (Tepleman, 14)
(100) A conviction [**based** on uncorroborated identification evidence] will be sustained in the absence of such a warning (Kingston, 14)
(101) Nothing **is gained** by the introduction of shifting burdens of proof … (Tepleman, 18)
(102) The conviction **must** be quashed (Dennis, 58)
(103) The jury **have to** consider … (Kingston, 18)
(104) They **are to** explain the reasons … (Kingston, 91)
(105) The proceeding should be dismissed on the grounds … (Tepleman, 138)
(106) His appeal **ought** to be dismissed (Smith, 315)
(107) … **see** the report of the decision of the Court of Appeal in 1978 (Whylie, 189)
(108) **Undoubtedly** … (Smith, 115)
(109) … **of course** … (Andrade, 65)
(110) He **was correct** | in saying | that **there is** no material distinction between the ones on a defendant … (Smith, 146–148)
(111) He **stressed** on more than one occasion | that mistakes **are made** in the identification of witnesses (Smith, 296-297)
(112) This observation **does** seem at variance with the judgment of the Court of Appeal (Andrade, 13)
(113) … that a case **does** come to trial at a proper speed (Tepleman, 123)

We can see the uncertain statement in the Russian language in the following signals: the combination of verbal categories—the Past Tense, Active Voice and Imperfective Aspect (example 114); combinations with determinants of “doubt” (example 115); references, explanations, quotations (example 116); interrogative sentences (example 117); subordinate clause of condition (example 118); conditional mood (example 119):

(114) На очной ставке подсудимый **давал** признательные показания. [At the confrontation the defendant **was making** a confession.] (Makhno, 29)

(115) Мне **почему-то** не думается … [**For some reason** I do not think …] (Koni, 868)

(116) Обязанность соблюдать законодательство о государственной тайне вытекает из общеправовой обязанности органов государственной власти, местного самоуправления, должностных лиц, граждан и их объединений соблюдать Конституцию Российской Федерации и законы (**статья 15, часть 2 Конституции РФ**) [The obligation to comply with the state secrecy laws is derived from the common law duty of public authorities, local self-government, officials, citizens and their associations to observe the Constitution and the laws of the Russian Federation (**Article 15, Part 2 of the Constitution of the Russian Federation**)] (Kondakov, 21)

(117) **За что была лишена жизни молодая женщина?** [**What has the young woman been deprived of life for?**] (Trukhanov, 649)

(118) **Если** он не причастен к преступлению … [**If** he is not involved in the crime …] (Abramov, 317)

(119) Мне **не было бы** надобности цитировать эти статьи … [It **would not be** necessary for me to quote these articles …] (Krassikov, 7)

As for the English language, the uncertain statement is actualised in these speech markers: the forms of the past tense (examples 120–121); present perfect (example 122); subjunctive mood (example 123); conditional mood (example 124); subordinate clause of condition (example 125); in an MSG with the meaning of probability, uncertainty expressed with the help of modal verbs such as “can” (example 126), “may” (example 127), the expression “to be likely + infinitive” (example 128); parenthetical words expressing uncertainty (example 129–130); constructions with "to seem/to appear" (example 131–132); interrogative sentences (example 133) and quotations (example 134). Look at some examples:

(120) He **had on** green khaki and **was holding** an M-16 rifle (Smith, 130–131)
(121) … who **had fallen** in the open gate-way (Dennis, 17)
(122) You **have heard** the statement … (Kingston, 111)
(123) **If** the constitutional rights of the applicant **had been infringed** by failing to try him within a reasonable time, | he **should not be obliged** to prepare for a retrial (Tepleman, 142–143)
(124) Certain fundamental rights [which **would** otherwise **exist** in law] are not taken away (Tepleman, 62)
(125) **If it is necessary** … (Tepleman, 80)
(126) That bullet **could** have come from either the left side or the right side (Reid, 126)
(127) It **may** not have been a voluntary statement. It **may** have been the result of violence or threats of violence (Smith, 240, 243)
(128) They **are likely to take** away the applicant′s right to the fair trial … (Kingston, 168)
(129) **Apparently** … (Whylie, 196)
(130) I **doubt** | they were there (Kingston, 45-46)
(131) That **seems** to be the irresistible inference … (Reid, 168)
(132) She **appears** not fully to have appreciated … (Reid, 81)
(133) **Why wait for the trial?** (Tepleman, 40)
(134) As the judgment emphasised | **"this passage gives too little weight to the dangers of convicting on uncorroborated evidence of identity"** (Andrade, 62–63)

Now we will turn our attention to the third implicit speech strategy "The sender's formation of addressee's attitude to a speech event by evaluation."

The implicit speech strategy "The sender's formation of addressee's attitude to a speech event by evaluation"

The implicit speech strategy "The sender's formation of addressee's attitude to a speech event by evaluation" is actualised with the help of three speech planes. They are:

- the plane of positive attitude
- the plane of neutral attitude
- the plane of negative attitude

This strategy deals with such a concept as "valuation of a speech event," closely connected to a definition "attitude." In linguistics, there are kinds of valuation (Fiodorova 1991, 49–50): (a) reproach, censure ("*Как тебе не стыдно!*" "*Ай-ай-ай!*") ["Shame on you!" "Ay-ay-ay!"]; (b) praise, approval ("*Молодец!*" "*Хорошо!*") ["Well done!" "Good!]; (c) accusation ("*Это ты натворил!*" "*Ты не прав.*") ["What have you done?" "You are wrong"]; (d) defence, justification ("*Ты не виноват.*" "*Ты правильно сделал.*") ["You are not to blame." "You did the right thing."] They are mostly directed to addressee's feelings and are based on the grounds of the generally accepted human moral criteria. The first two kinds, reproach/ censure and praise/approval, apply to a moral-ethic sphere, and the last two, accusation and defence/justification, imply a social-legal sphere of behavioural valuation. The speech for the prosecution which is under review applies to a social-legal sphere of behavioural valuation—prosecution. Before turning to characterisation of the prosecutors' valuation it will be reasonable to study its structure.

The structure of valuation consists of the following four components (Ivin 1970, 27): **A subject of valuation** means an estimating person. **An object of valuation** is an object or a phenomenon which is the purposes of the subject's attitude. **A ground of valuation** is that position and those reasons which make subjects praise, reproach or feel neutral attitude to different things and events. **Character of valuation** implies positive or negative characteristics of a definite thing.

In our case, a subject of valuation is a complex formation which includes the public prosecutor themself and their addressee—the audience, perceiving the prosecutor's speech, which is to reach a verdict. The main object of evaluation is the defendant's illegal actions which have caused negative effects, and the personality of the defendant themself. The grounds of valuation refer to the rational point (evidence, specific facts, the force of logic), and the character of evaluation to the emotional moment (positive or negative characteristics of the objects of evaluation).

Positive or negative evaluation can be expressed explicitly and implicitly. When there is an explicit evaluation of positive or negative attitude to the object, the meanings of linguistic units are used directly. Implicit evaluation is characterised by the absence of an evaluative attitude of the speaker to denotatum in the structure of the semantics, expressed with the help of various connotations, contextual and other distributional characteristics of the object. Explicit expression of evaluation is more typical in the speeches for the prosecution during the period of the so-called "building of socialism" in the USSR. These speeches contain an open negative evaluation and are full of not only negative emotional-expressive vocabulary, but even invectives which have the intention of insulting or humiliating the defendant.

The system of evaluative meanings is based on two main signs—"good" and "bad." These meanings good/bad are on the scale of evaluation where there are zones of positive and negative. Between them is a neutral zone where signs of good/bad are in a certain balance. Movement on this scale from good to bad is according to different parameters. It is based on a combination of social and individual, stereotypes of values and worldview and the subjective attitude of the individual to the appropriate object based on the idea of pleasant/unpleasant, on what they like and dislike, and so on (Volf 1986, 98–100).

As stated above, the signs of evaluation also depend on the worldview of the society. It is interesting to note that the words of political language have a basically polemical meaning. Such words as "a republic," "a class," "a legal state," "dictatorship" and so on are still unclear on if it is known exactly who should be "struck," "beaten" or "subjected to denial" by such words. Each of the opponents using the same words puts into them a completely opposite meaning (Pocheptsov 2001, 218). Let us compare:

(135) *На Россию они стали смотреть не как на отечество, а как на объект* ***социально-революционных*** *мероприятий* [They began to look at Russia not as at their homeland but as an object of **social-revolutionary** activities] (Muraviov, 294)

(136) *Наши учителя Маркс и Энгельс 50 лет назад предсказали, в какой роли должны будут выступить те или иные общественные группировки в период* ***социальной революции.*** [Fifty years ago our teachers Marx and Engels predicted in what roles the certain social groups would act in the period of the **social revolution**] (Lunacharskiy, 14–15)

Taking into account the socio-political situation of the end of the nineteenth and the beginning of the twentieth century in Russia, and the ideological position of public prosecutors of the relevant periods, we can only conclude that in Example 135 the author creates the listeners' negative attitude to the speech event and in Example 136 forms the positive attitude.

Explicit evaluation expressed by a public prosecutor sometimes antagonises as a listener feels that it is forcing their decision. Freedom, including freedom of decision-making, is one of the basic human values, and that is why the task of the prosecutor at the trial is to make the listener have the impression that their decision was made of their own free will. Judges, especially jurors, like all people are different by nature and have their own values and models of behaviour. A professionally successful public prosecutor understands that they are not to rely only on themself in the process of persuasive communication, but should be guided by the values and needs of their audience. Therefore, from the psychological point of view, for a successful influence on an addressee a public prosecutor should satisfy any of the listener's requirements or needs.

In psychology, the problem of needs began to be studied more and more in the twentieth century. Presently, there are many definitions of "needs" based on the explanation of their nature: as poverty (Uznadze 1982); as the lack of good, as value (Magun 1983; Maslow 1954, 1967); as a necessity (Lomov 1999; Dodonov 1978, 1987; Leontiev 1982, 1984), etc. We will study one of the most developed and diverse classifications of needs proposed by Abraham Maslow (1967: 93–127). According to this hierarchy, human needs fall into the following five areas.

(1) **Biological and physiological needs**—air, food, drink, shelter, warmth, sex, sleep, etc. These are biological and consist of needs for oxygen, food, water and a relatively constant body temperature. They are the strongest needs because if a person were deprived of all needs, the physiological ones would come first in the search for satisfaction. As a rule, this type of need for a modern person is satisfied. Therefore, public prosecutors in implicit influence are turning to more complex types of needs. However, at the beginning of the twentieth century when in Russia everywhere there was devastation and hunger dominated, physiological needs came first and were intuitively used by the state prosecutors. The following are examples from the speech of the public prosecutor Pokrovskiy:

(137) *Осенью 1936 года враги оставили под снегом 7 тысяч гектаров хлеба. Весной этого года не досеяли 5 700 гектаров* (36–37) [In the autumn of 1936 the enemies left in the snow 7,000 hectares of grain. In the spring of this year they left without sowing 5,700 hectares] (36–37)

(138) *Партия и правительство заботятся, чтобы у каждого колхозника была корова* (43–44) [The party and the

government are eager for every collective farmer to have a cow] (43–44)

(139) *Колхозы Курагинского района на основе последних решений правительства получили огромные льготы: списаны недоимки, снижены нормы хлебопоставок. 70 тысяч центнеров зерна дополнительно получают курагинские колхозники на свои трудодни. Страна уже в этом году добилась получения 7 миллиардов пудов хлеба* (20–24) [Based on the latest government's decisions the collective farms of Kuraginskiy district got huge benefits: written off arrears, lower standards of bread delivery. Kuraginskiy farmers additionally receive 70, 000 quintals of grain for their labour. The country has already made getting 7 billion tons of grain this year] (20–24)

The state prosecutor is forming a negative attitude toward the defendant using both the negative aspects of the methods of so-called "wrecking work" ("вредительская работа-vreditelskaya rabota") (example 137) and the positive aspects of the care of the Communist Party and government for the welfare of farmers (examples 138 and 139). We see that in all these examples the state prosecutor in an implicit form touches upon the physiological needs of his addressee for a successful influence.

(2) **Safety needs**—protection from elements, security, order, law, limits, stability, etc. When all physiological needs are satisfied and are no longer controlling thoughts and behaviours, the needs for security can become active. Adults have little awareness of their security needs except in times of emergency or periods of disorganisation in the social structure (such as widespread rioting). Children often display the signs of insecurity and the need to be safe. This is the second kind of primary needs expressed in the desire to feel safe, to get rid of the failures and fears. This kind of need is actual for all mankind and especially for Russia at all stages of its development. Russian people have always felt the need for stability, order, the predictability of events. To meet security needs, a sense of fear as a target of influence is often intuitively used by public prosecutors, and can be attained with the help of exaggeration:

(140) *Материалы дела просто «кричат» о состоянии нашего общества.* [The materials of the case are just "screaming" about the state of our society.] (Romanov, 12)

(141) *Настоящий процесс дал огромный материал, охватить который в речи одного обвинителя нет возможности.* [This process gave a huge amount of material which is not possible to cover in the speech of the prosecutor] (Lunacharskiy, 1–2)

Presently, one can see exaggeration in almost every criminal trial in Russia. A prosecutor can use it when they see the weakness of the evidence and warns everybody that they will worry about their wives and children if the defendant is acquitted. In addition, to meet safety needs, the judges will just have to protect society, and especially themselves, from the defendant.

(3) **Belongingness and love needs**—work group, family, affection, relationships, etc. When the needs for safety and for physiological well-being are satisfied, the next class of needs for love, affection and belongingness can emerge. Maslow states that people seek to overcome feelings of loneliness and alienation. This involves both giving and receiving love, affection and the sense of belonging.

These are secondary needs based on the sense of belonging to anything or anyone, on a sense of affection and support. We love and we are likely to be loved by people who are like us, and on the contrary, we do not love and we are not loved by people who so much differ from us. Why is this so? Firstly, the higher the level of agreement the easier it is to predict the behaviour of another person. Secondly, the more similar the setups of an addresser and an addressee are, the stronger the feeling of reality and significance of their views, which is essential for maintaining self-confidence and improving self-identity. Tension caused by differences of views creates discomfort which a person tries to dispel by aligning their behaviour with that of another person. This basic motivation was named "the need for consensus," and is reflected in people trying to increase the significance of their views by aligning them with other people (Kunitsyna 2002, 203–204).

The audience at the trial consists of people who are not united by a common interest before the process, so such an interest has to be created. Here, an experienced state prosecutor on the unconscious level uses the needs of an addressee in the social interaction actualising in his speech the inclusive "we" and its forms:

(142) ***Мы*** *рассмотрели* ***с вами*** *все обстоятельства.* [**We** have studied **together** all the circumstances] (Fiodorov, 211)

(143) *Эта статья подводит **нас** к статье 57 Уголовного кодекса.* [This article brings **us** to Article 57 of the Criminal Code] (Krassikov, 18)

"We" expresses an interaction between a speaker and their audience, it creates the effect of communication and personal contact between them. Thus, the state prosecutor invites the judges to the joint reflection, creates an atmosphere of a relaxed conversation and creates a sense of trust between the prosecutor and the court.

The addressee's trust can be caused by well-known (to the definite community) quotations, catchphrases, proverbs and sayings. It is easier for a speaker to create the necessary attitude to the object of evaluation on the grounds of such expressions:

(144) ***Как черт от ладана**, Бухарин бежит от признания своей вины.* [**Like the devil from holy water**, Bukharin runs from acknowledging his guilt] (Vyshinskiy, 197)
(145) ***Белыми нитками шиты** все эти заявления о революционном геройстве.* [Every barber knows (in the Russian variant it sounds like: "it is sewed with a white thread," so this saying has the meaning "it is transparent, obvious, poorly disguised") all these statements about the revolutionary heroism] (Muraviov, 422)

Moreover, the transformation of these expressions increases the effecting influence and the power of what has been said (Zyubina 2001, 203–206). Such transformed expressions cause surprising, and surprise is the first act of cognition. A person is surprised when they have to face not a new phenomenon but one which they have mistakenly believed fully known. We will give some examples of such individual transformations:

(146) *Эта сумма – **капля в море долгов и претензий**.* [This amount is **a drop in the sea of debts and claims**.] (Koni, 847)
(147) *... **министр иностранных дел без портфеля** рассказывал ...* [... **the Foreign Minister without portfolio** told ...] (Lunacharskiy, 539)

However, speaking about rare citations or quotations and poorly understood expressions, we can tell that in contrast they cause irritation not only to jurors who are generally of low educational level (at least in Russia) but also to professional judges. To my mind, it happens because in the context of common everyday circumstances of the trial case, such references often seem to be out of place and they will rather indicate the speaker's wish of using an occasion to show his eloquence and erudition, but in no way will cause the sympathies of listeners and most importantly will not increase the number of supporters of his views (Romanov 2001, 468).

Asking questions is another manifestation of social interaction between an addresser and an addressee. Questions stimulate the thinking of a listener and make one listen to a speaker more attentively:

> (148) *Действительно ли виновен Будков во взрыве? Или это сделал кто-нибудь другой из недругов Караичева?* [Is Budkov really guilty in the explosion? Or did someone else from the enemies of Karaichev do it?] (Trukhanov, 99–100)

Especially valuable for the influence on the listener is a rhetorical question, that is a statement in the form of a question:

> (149) *Разве получила бы мать Тищенко такие льготы? Но может ли тяжесть положения семьи Тищенко оправдать его действия?* [Could the mother of Tishchenko have received such benefits? But can the plight of Tishchenko's family justify his actions?] (Melnikov, 123 and 127)

What is the secret of effectiveness when we are asking a rhetorical question? It is connected to the peculiarities of our hormonal system. When we say "yes" it means agreement, and moreover it means the realisation that in the near future there will not be any confrontation with this person. Our body, orienting to the economical consumption of power, immediately relaxes with the help of adding endorphins to our blood, which are more often called "hormones of pleasure" (Sheinov 2001, 308). Thus, a state prosecutor with a few uses of "yes" makes the judge relax, and can significantly reduce their will to resist in the question of the defendant's guilt.

Social needs are also involved when a state prosecutor uses quotations from famous persons. People are flattered when they share something, even if it is only a common vision, with great and famous people. Such references often do not relate to the subject matter. Especially often, we observe this phenomenon in the speeches of public prosecutors of the beginning of the twentieth century in the USSR. They use almost every opportunity to mention the classics of Marxism-Leninism:

(150) *Наши учителя* ***Маркс*** *и* ***Энгельс*** *пятьдесят лет назад предсказали …* [Fifty years ago our teachers **Marx** and **Engels** predicted …] (Lunacharskiy, 14)

Even just a single mention of these powerful names was enough for a successful influence on the audience.

(4) **Esteem needs**—self-esteem, achievement, mastery, independence, status, dominance, prestige, managerial responsibility, etc. When the first three classes of needs are satisfied, the needs for esteem can become dominant. These involve needs for both self-esteem and for esteem a person gets from others. Humans have a need for a stable, firmly based, high level of self-respect, and respect from others. When these needs are satisfied, the person feels self-confident and valuable as a person in the world. When these needs are frustrated, the person feels inferior, weak, helpless and worthless.

Knowing that somebody likes us turns out to be a kind of reward that increases our self-esteem. Even a mere expression of interest to an individual is a hidden compliment to this person: it is pleasant for everyone to feel confirmation of the self-worth. Therefore, a state prosecutor often directly addresses the audience actualising in his speech an address to the audience, exclusive "you" and its forms, which, of course, implicitly affect the listener:

(151) ***Товарищи судьи революционного трибунала!*** (***Comrades Judges of the Revolutionary Tribunal!***) (Krassikov, 1)
(152) *А теперь, с* ***вашего*** *позволения …* [*And now with* ***your*** *permission …*] (Melnikov, 6)

Also to be considered, as a kind of manifestation of respect for the judicial audience, is the use of documentary evidence (exact figures, results of various examinations, references to competent sources, testimony of witnesses). Whenever we see documentary evidence we feel confidence in the material as a whole. By sharing this information, a public prosecutor declines judges on their side, showing respect for the intellectual capacity of the judicial audience. Use of numerical data is of great importance here. A few impressive figures can serve as a powerful argument which will be very difficult to disprove, and the secret advantage is in the fact that it is rather difficult to verify such materials at the same time and place. For the persuasiveness in the convincingness of the figures, one should read them aloud (not just speak out) to leave no shadow of doubt in their authenticity. The second way to use figures is radically opposite in its targets. It is based on the fact that a great number of figures is perceived badly, and is too difficult to understand. Therefore, some speakers throw onto a listener a waterfall of numbers with the aim of confusing an addressee and to show a "serious argumentation" (Sheinov 2001, 321). Some examples:

> (153) *Если **в 1991 г.** было зарегистрировано **16 122** умышленных убийства, то **в 1998 году** таких преступлений было уже **29 551**, а **в 2001 г.**—свыше **30 тыс** ...* [*If **in 1991** there were **16,122** murders, **in 1998** there were already **29,551** such crimes, and **in 2001**—more than **30 thousand** ...*) (Abramov, 14–16)
> (154) *За два года пребывания в районе вредители выжили из колхозов **1 326** колхозных дворов. На первое января 1936 года в районе было **8 114** рабочих лошадей. Из них осталось на первое января 1937 года только **6 652**. Чудинов за один год погубил **512** голов скота, оставил под снегом **255** гектаров хлеба.* [*For the two years in the area the saboteurs have got rid of **1,326** farm collective households. On the January 1, 1936 there were **8,114** working horses in the district. And only **6,652** of them remained on the 1st of January in 1937. For one year Chudinov killed **512** head of cattle, and he left in the snow **255** hectares of corn*] (Pokrovskiy, 39–41, 81–82)

This stream of figures only creates the impression of probative value of the speech, but in fact the addressee is not able to perceive and remember such information. Thus, the public prosecutor uses the magic of figures as a means of implicit control of his audience.

(5) **Self-actualisation needs**—realising personal potential, self-fulfilment, seeking personal growth and peak experiences. When all of the foregoing needs are satisfied, then and only then are the needs for self-actualisation activated. Maslow describes self-actualisation as a person's need to be and do that which they were "born to do." For example, a musician must make music, an artist must paint, and a poet must write. These needs make themselves felt in signs of restlessness. The person feels on edge, tense, lacking something, in short, restless. If a person is hungry, unsafe, not loved or accepted, or lacking self-esteem, it is very easy to know what the person is restless about. It is not always clear what a person wants when there is a need for self-actualisation.

Self-actualisation is one of the most individualised needs. What is natural for one can be completely incomprehensible to someone else. This form of needs is the easiest way to influence an individual, but not for such a diverse audience as the judiciary, and especially not for the jurors. Nevertheless, one can still identify some general points concerning the self-actualisation of a person.

Self-actualisation is manifested in achievements (Sheinov 2001, 25). Therefore, a person is always pleased to receive any confirmation of their success, even if in the future:

> (155) *Дело за вашим решением... Уверен, что оно будет объективным и справедливым* [It depends on your decision … I am sure it will be objective and fair] (Abramov, 434, 436–437).

In this example, the public prosecutor treats the jurors as unique individuals with high moral and intellectual qualities, and in most cases jurors are trying to live up to their trust. An experienced public prosecutor uses confidence in the abilities of the addressee in order to influence them latently. We see that considering the personal needs of the judges is an important factor in the hidden influence in the speech of a public prosecutor.

Thus, the markers of the planes of the formation of a positive and a negative attitude to a speech event are explicit and implicit actualisation of lexical units containing a positive or negative evaluation. The markers of the plane of forming a neutral attitude to a speech event is the absence of evaluative lexical means (both explicit and implicit ones).

The next stage of the pragmalinguistic experiment is the selection of the public prosecutors' speeches. For the analysis, it is reasonable to use texts which are as close as possible in their content and structure. In other words, the texts must have the greatest possible number of common features in order to define the studied differences. Since we are studying the speech behaviour of an individual, an extremely subjective category, it is insufficient to have just the same structure of the texts, and an important condition for selection is psychological and biological similarity between the authors, as well as the similarity of their social experience.

In accordance with these requirements, we compared texts that are relatively homogeneous, and took into account:

- one speech genre, that is the speech for the prosecution (and moreover, speeches concerning only criminal cases were analysed)
- synchronous periods (the public prosecutors' speeches of the end of the nineteenth century, of the 1920s to 1940s and of the beginning of the twenty-first century were separately studied)

- the nationality of the authors (Russian- and English-speaking prosecutors)
- gender of the authors (all state prosecutors are male)
- addressees (the speeches for professional judges and the jurors were studied separately).

As a result, we have selected texts of the speeches for the prosecution of:

- seven Russian-speaking public prosecutors for the jury at the end of the nineteenth century
- seven Russian-speaking public prosecutors for the professional court in the 1920s to 1940s
- seven Russian-speaking public prosecutors for the jury at the beginning of the nineteenth century
- seven Russian-speaking public prosecutors for the professional court at the beginning of the twenty-first century, and
- seven English-speaking public prosecutors for the jury at the beginning of the twenty-first century.

For the greater objectivity, in Part I (Point 4) we studied the speech behaviour of a public prosecutor Trukhanov in the texts of different genres: a speech for the professional court, a speech for the jury, and an article on a criminal law theme for the newspaper *Vecherniy Rostov/Evening Rostov*.

Then there was preparation of the texts for the analysis. The chosen texts were divided into minor syntactic groups—MSG. The main criterion for dividing a text into MSGs is the presence of predicativity and modality in the utterance.

From the standpoint of Pragmalinguistics, predicativity and modality are the common features of any statement expressed by any sentence. A unit of Pragmalinguistic study is MSG, which in terms of Pragmatics is a syntactical actualisation of a speech act in a text, according to the model of a speech act, which is represented in the following scheme: the addresser—the message—the addressee (Matveeva, Nuzhnova, Tonchenko 2001, 190—197). An MSG is a basic unit of study in the pragmalinguistic experiment.

21,760 MSGs were analysed according to three implicit speech strategies: "Participation/Nonparticipation of members of communication in a speech event," "Sure/Unsure speech behaviour of an author" and "The sender's formation of addressee's attitude to a speech event by evaluation" (a total of 65,280 MSGs).

Matrix 1: The analysis of the sender's text according to the implicit speech strategy "Participation/Nonparticipation of members of communication in a speech event"

№ of MSG	the plane of *personal* participation	the plane of *social* participation	the plane of *objective* participation
1.	+		
2.		+	
3.			+

Matrix 2: The analysis of the sender's text according to the implicit speech strategy "Sure/Unsure speech behaviour of an author"

№ of MSG	*certain* statement	*uncertain* statement
1.	+	
2.		+
3.	+	

Matrix 3: The analysis of the sender's text according to the implicit speech strategy "The sender's formation of addressee's attitude to a speech event by evaluation"

№ of MSG	the plane of *positive* attitude	the plane of *neutral* attitude	the plane of *negative* attitude
1.	+		
2.		+	
3.			+

The next phase is making the analysis. We looked for the speech signals in the text and fixed them in the above matrices, and a quantitative calculation of speech signals actualised by the authors was made, the frequency of which was counted according to the formula:

$$F \text{ of the plane} = \frac{\Sigma \text{ MSG of the plane x 100 percent}}{\Sigma \text{ MSG of the text}}, \text{ where}$$

F of the plane is the frequency of the plane in percent,
Σ is the sum of all the MSGs of a plane or a text (Matveeva, 1999: 58).

Finally, for each strategy the average speech-genre index was calculated, deviations from which have a diagnosing nature. On the basis of deviations from the average speech-genre index we are able to make an interpretation of the authors' speech portraits and to make a diagnosis of their personal qualities.

Now we will study the results of the pragmalinguistic experiment to identify individual features of the Russian-speaking and English-speaking public prosecutors and the stereotypical speech behaviour of these groups.

2. Russian-speaking prosecutors' speech behaviour in different periods of history before different addressees

2.1. Russian-speaking prosecutors' speech behaviour at the end of the nineteenth century before a trial by jury

Let us study the fragments of speech portraits of Russian-speaking public prosecutors speaking for the jury at the end of the nineteenth century, according to three implicit speech strategies: "Participation/ Nonparticipation of members of communication in a speech event," "Sure/Unsure speech behaviour of an author" and "The sender's formation of addressee's attitude to a speech event by evaluation." In accordance with these strategies, we have analysed 4,994 MSGs and created table 2 (see appendix). Now we will identify some individual-personal features of the public prosecutors in accordance with the above mentioned strategies.

The implicit speech strategy "Participation/Nonparticipation of members of communication in a speech event"

According to the study of the seven speeches for the prosecution, the average speech-genre index of the plane of personal participation is 12.4 percent (see table 2). This is the average speech-genre index, and is the indicator of the standard behaviour of the author in the genre of the speech for the prosecution at the end of the nineteenth century in Russia. However, the indicators diagnosing the individual-personal features of a personality will be higher or lower than this average speech-genre index.

Most frequently, the markers of the plane of personal participation are used by K. I. Kessel (24 percent), M. G. Kazarinov (20.4 percent) and A. I. Urussov (17 percent). The frequent actualisation of this plane shows that the authors are leaders by nature. They are active, initiative, resourceful and sharp-witted. Moreover, they have some traits of authoritarianism and egocentrism. A high rate of the plane of personal participation reveals a person with high self-esteem, which, in its turn, indicates the tendency to "narcissism" (Dilts 2001, 48). Thus, for example, contemporaries remarked on the presence of morbid pride in Kessel's character (Koni 1968, 84).

The indicators below the average speech-genre index of the plane of personal participation (12.4 percent) are observed in Koni's (7.2 percent) and Zhukov's (8.2 percent) speech behaviours, and the rate close to the average speech-genre index in Plevako's behaviour (10.5 percent). It indicates the authors' modesty, their desire not to put themselves first, and the absence of authoritarianism.

In this regard, it is interesting to recollect the words of Koni about Urussov and Plevako (Koni 1968, 123–124). He mentions that these two outstanding masters of lawyer's eloquence were completely different people. Urussov was a little arrogant, and, in the midst of the judicial debate, it seemed that he condescended to his opponent, and lit up the painful pages of the case with some kind of disgust. But Plevako was a "democrat-raznochinets" (a person not of noble birth) who knew life at all the levels of Russian society. He was always a person of ready sympathy, kind-hearted and unpretentious.

Regarding the actualisation of the plane of social participation, we should say that it can be correlated with the cooperative type of behaviour when an addressee is influenced by the automatic mechanism of convincing, which is based on a sense of imitation and psychological cooperation. The average speech-genre index of the plane of social participation is 7.6 percent, so indicators which are higher or lower than the average speech-genre index will be diagnosing.

More often, we find the markers of this plane in Kessel's (14.7 percent) and Muraviov's (12 percent) speeches for the prosecution. Such a high index of the social plane of Kessel, combined with even a higher level of the personal plane (see above), indicates an unconscious desire to dominate the addressee. In contrast, the high index of the social plane in the speeches of Muraviov shows that the prosecutor can establish emotional contacts with the various parties of communication, and has the ability to cooperate with different people. He is friendly and knows how to listen to his interlocutor. According to the memoirs of contemporaries, the speeches of Muraviov were impeccable—they were legally grounded, passionate and always attracted listeners. People often came to the court with the only purpose to listen to the talented master of lawyer's eloquence (Zvyagintsev 2001, 174).

The indices of the other five addressers (Zhukov 7 percent; Kazarinov 7 percent; Koni 6.5 percent; Plevako 6 percent; Urussov 6 percent) did not differ substantially from the average index of the social plane (7.6 percent), and thus are not revealing.

Now we will study the data of the plane of objective participation, which significantly predominates these texts. The average index of this plane is 80 percent, meaning that the public prosecutors automatically focused their attention on the objective sides of the criminal acts. Thus, the listeners feel confident in the given facts.

More often, the plane of objective participation is actualised in the texts of Koni (86.3 percent) and Zhukov (84.8 percent). They say that an important feature of Koni's speeches for the prosecution was a consistent and thorough review of evidence. His speeches were not limited to the narrow frames of a definite case. He almost always, in one way or another, touched upon the problems of criminal or criminal-procedural law. Koni had a great wealth of knowledge, a keen and observant mind, strict logical thinking and a gift of broad generalisation of facts (Vydrya 1967, 10). The high rates of the plane of objective participation suggest that the authors had an inherent tendency to concentrate on the objective circumstances of the cases, on the very essence of the matter. These prosecutors had a clear logic, a talent for organisation and clarity of presentation at the court.

More rarely one can find the plane of objective participation in the texts of Kessel's (61.3 percent), Kazarinov's (72.6 percent) and Muraviov's (75 percent) speeches. To my mind, the main reason for this fact is that for these public prosecutors the factual side of the case is not as important as the emotional-subjective manifestation, which will be described further.

The implicit speech strategy "Sure/Unsure speech behaviour of an author"

This strategy is actualised in the texts with the help of two speech planes: the first is a certain statement and the second is an uncertain statement, which correlate with confident and unsure kinds of speech behaviour of the author respectively. Both sure and cautious statements have the goal of persuasion (Matveeva 1993, 201). In the process of convincing, the main factor is the authority of the speaker in the eyes of the listener. It consists of the sender's confidence in the success of his influence on the addressee.

Let us study the data given in table 2 (see appendix). As shown by the material of our study, the average speech-genre index of the plane of the certain statement in the court speech for the prosecution is 40.6 percent, and the indicators which are higher or lower than this index will diagnose personal traits.

We can see the highest rates of the certain statement in the speeches of Kessel (60 percent) and Muraviov (56 percent). The frequent use of this plane's speech signals indicates such an individual personal trait as confidence in oneself and in one's own actions. A confident person has such personal qualities as initiative, self-reliance, independence, decisiveness, courage, perseverance, endurance and adherence to one's own principles (Rubinshtein 1999, 20), and Kessel's and Muraviov's characters probably had these qualities.

The low percentage of the certain statement (in the speeches of Koni it is 34.2 percent and in those of Urussov 35.1 percent), compared with the average speech-genre index (40.6 percent), indicates the uncertainty and caution of the authors. Koni and Urussov have such an individual-personal quality as precaution. They are restrained in their manifestations, indecisive, often unsure. Such people are usually trying to plan their actions several steps ahead, to estimate the pros and cons before acting, as they feel very uncomfortable if they fail (Nuzhnova 2003, 85). Low actualisation of categorical data in the texts of these prosecutors delivering their speeches in court shows that their speeches are ethically restrained—"they do not exacerbate the difficulties and misfortunes of people by public mockery" (Enikeev 1996, 274).

We cannot diagnose the personal qualities of the other state prosecutors because the level of their categorical statement is almost identical to the average speech-genre index (the difference is only 0.8 percent to 1.1 percent).

The implicit speech strategy "The sender's formation of addressee's attitude to a speech event by evaluation"

This strategy is realised in a text through three speech planes. They are: (a) the plane of positive attitude; (b) the plane of neutral attitude; and (c) the plane of negative attitude. We will now analyse the proportions of speech signals, studying each plane of the implicit speech strategy "the sender's formation of addressee's attitude to a speech event by evaluation" and carry out the diagnosis of some individual personal qualities of public prosecutors of the end of the nineteenth century.

According to the results of the study, the average speech-genre index of this strategy (43 percent) is much bigger than that of attitude (11 percent). Therefore, it will be more reasonable to start our analysis by considering the plane of forming the addressee's negative attitude to a speech event.

We can mark out a few public prosecutors in whose speeches the signals of this plane are found more often than in 50 percent of the texts. They are Kazarinov (55.9 percent), Muraviov (52.6 percent) and Koni (50.2 percent). These indices indicate pessimism in the worldview of the authors of the texts.

Pessimism is defined as emphasising or thinking of the bad part of a situation rather than the good, or the feeling that bad things are more likely to happen than good. A person in a dismal mood does not believe in the future, tending to see only the unpleasant in everything (Ozhegov 1997, 428). On the other hand, pessimists are capable of deep empathy, emotional warmth, a responsive and kind attitude. Thus, according to the memoirs of contemporaries, Koni's main personal features were warmth, intimacy, a subtle understanding of the movements of a human soul, and the ability to give a correct analysis of human actions (Porubov 2001, 32).

Moreover, Koni actualises the signals of forming the positive attitude to a speech event by evaluation more often than many other public prosecutors. Compared to the average speech-genre index of forming the positive attitude (11 percent) he actualises this plane in 14.8 percent of the cases. An even higher index we can see only in Kazarinov's speeches, at 21.9 percent. Of course, by such low rates of this plane we cannot judge the optimism of these state prosecutors of the end of the nineteenth century, but we can conclude that in comparison with the other authors they see not only negative aspects of a crime.

According to contemporaries, in speeches for the prosecution Koni repeatedly drew the attention of jurors to the need of mitigating the punishment for the defendants. Being a great humanist, he was always able to find warm heartfelt words and bright memorable colours for an explanation of deep human emotions. However, the humanity of Koni did not mean sentimentality and feebleness. His words resounded angrily when discussing the events of great public importance (Vydrya 1967, 15–16). Such traits as emotional responsiveness, moral purity and the constant desire to defend the truth were combined in Koni's character (Volk, Vydrya and Muratov 1966, 31).

The lowest index of the positive attitude (5 percent) belongs to Kessel. His speeches for the prosecution seemed colourless, weak and watery (Koni 1966, 84). His index of neutral attitude (49.5 percent) is higher than the average speech-genre index (46 percent). It was due to the fact that his speech was monotonous and mostly made up of dry abstract bookish expressions, and the greatest part of his speech was devoted to studying the details of the crime and preparation for it (Mikhailovskaya 1981, 87).

What is more, the signals of the plane of positive attitude to the speech event by evaluation are also rarely actualised by Muraviov (5.4 percent) if we compare them with the average speech-genre index which is 11 percent. This indicator, combined with the high amount of the signals of the plane of negative attitude to the speech event by evaluation (see above), indicates the strongly pronounced pessimistic mood of Muraviov.

Another example of an emotional fighter for truth was Plevako. Giving priority to the factors of psychological impact, he believed that logic is logic, but it is a human being in the court, and to prove does not mean to persuade (Rechi 1985, 5). The power of Plevako's speeches over the audience was infinite. He penetrated into the souls of the people. According to the memoirs of contemporaries, there was no more typical court speaker in Russia than Plevako (Porubov 2001, 33). It is interesting to take note of the fact that Plevako, in all three studied strategies, intuitively used sets of markers of the respective planes which are close to the respective average speech-genre indices. We will give a list of these correlations, indicating in parentheses the average speech-genre index: the plane of personal participation—10.5 percent (12.4 percent); the plane of social participation—6 percent (7.6 percent); the plane of objective participation—83.5 percent (80 percent); the plane of certain statement—41.4 percent (40.6 percent); the plane of uncertain statement—58.6 percent (59.4 percent), the plane of positive attitude—9.9 percent (11 percent); the plane of neutral attitude—45.7 percent (46 percent); the plane of negative attitude—44.4 percent (43 percent). Thus, Plevako intuitively followed an unwritten stereotyped speech behaviour of the group of prosecutors of the nineteenth century, and it helped him to psychologically influence the jurors.

We have diagnosed some individual personal qualities of the public prosecutors of Russia at the end of the nineteenth century, studying their speech behaviour at the trial by jury. Let us turn to the next group of the public prosecutors.

2.2. Russian-speaking prosecutors' speech behaviour in the USSR in the 1920s to 1940s before a professional trial

Now we will study the fragments of Russian-speaking prosecutors' speech behaviour in the USSR in the 1920s to 1940s before a professional trial, according to three implicit speech strategies: "Participation/Nonparticipation of members of communication in a speech event," "Sure/Unsure speech behaviour of an author" and "The sender's formation of addressee's attitude to a speech event by evaluation." Let us now identify some individual-personal features of these public prosecutors. In accordance with these strategies, we have analysed 4,793 MSGs and created table 3 (see appendix).

The implicit speech strategy "Participation/Nonparticipation of members of communication in a speech event"

According to table 3, created with the results of the study of seven speeches for the prosecution, the average speech-genre index of the plane of personal participation is 10 percent. This is the average speech-genre index, the indicator of unwritten standard for the genre of speeches for the prosecution in the 1920s to 1940s before a professional trial. However, the indicators diagnosing the individual-personal features of a personality will be the indicators which are higher or lower than this average speech-genre index.

The most frequent actualisation of the plane of personal participation can be seen in the speeches for the prosecution of Koni (22.1 percent) and Krylenko (17 percent). As we know, Krylenko had a high position in government: he was the prosecutor of the RSFSR (Russian Soviet Federative Socialistic Republic), the head of the People's Commissariat of Justice of the RSFSR and then of the Soviet Union. As a state prosecutor, Krylenko took part in all the major political processes, as well as in some of the processes that were very important because of their social value or were devoted to the fight against economic dislocation in the RSFSR (Ivakina 1995, 31). People who have a higher plane of personal participation than the average speech-genre index (10 percent), such as Koni (22.1 percent) and Krylenko (17 percent) are distinguished by such individual personal traits as authoritarianism, courage, determination and independence. What is more, Krylenko's contemporaries noted that he was a man of exuberant nature, principled, uncompromising and straightforward (Zaitsev 1977, 102).

The indicators less than the average speech-genre index (10 percent) are observed in the speeches for the prosecution of Lunacharskiy (2.5 percent), Pokrovskiy (4.5 percent) and Vyshinskiy (5.6 percent). It indicates the low self-esteem of all these authors. That is why they do not seek or fear (taking into account the political situation in the USSR in that period) to show their individuality.

The average speech-genre index of the plane of social participation is 13.6 percent. We see the signals of this plane in the speeches for the prosecution of Krassikov (29.7 percent) and Lunacharskiy (20 percent) more often than in the speeches of the other addressers. The authors who have a high level on the social plane have a cooperative type of behaviour. These public prosecutors act in accordance with the idea familiar to whole generations of Soviet people: "who is not with us is against us" (Vitsin 1999, 11). There is one thing to note: Krassikov also actualises his personal participation in a speech event, thus not pulling away from the facts given by him (his index of the plane of personal participation is 9.7 percent, so is almost equal to the average speech-genre index of this plane, 10 percent), but Lunacharskiy on the contrary does not want to be morally responsible for his own words (his index of the plane of personal participation is very low in this case at 2.5 percent).

It should be noted that during the period being studied, instead of laws there was in force a so called "revolutionary sense of justice." Decisions of the courts did not even subject to appeal (Mikhlin 1997, 35). The low levels of the social plane of the speeches made by Kondrushkin (6.9 percent) and Vyshinskiy (7.9 percent) indicate that these prosecutors did not have any sense of collectivism. We cannot say that these authors have such individual personal qualities as responsiveness and sympathy, friendliness, open-heartedness, cheerfulness, optimism and carelessness (Kjell, Ziengler, 1997, 317).

Now we will turn to the plane of objective participation. The average speech-genre index of this plane is 76.4 percent. The predominance of the plane of objective participation in the speeches for the prosecution in this period is explained by the fact that in the Soviet state a criminal prosecution process was only a form of cover for the opponents' reprisal. The state prosecutors with high indices of objective participation (Pokrovskiy 87 percent; Vyshinskiy 86.5 percent; Kondrushkin 86.3 percent) did not even consider it necessary to convince their listeners that they were right due to the lack of adversarial proceedings, listing only the "evil deeds" of the defendants, almost without expressing their personal attitude. From the psychological point of view, one can say that Pokrovskiy, Vyshinskiy and Kondrushkin are people characterised by focus on inanimate objects. In psychology, such people are called "introverts" (Egorova 1997, 47). They are calm, assertive, reserved, closed. Introverts tend towards introspective reflection, do not laugh very often and have depressive tendencies. They never get bored with themselves, and they tend to be solitary (Kunitsyna, Kazarinova and Pogolsha 2002, 427).

The implicit speech strategy "Sure/Unsure speech behaviour of an author"

The average speech-genre index of the plane of certain statement is 43.5 percent. The largest deviations upwards from the average speech-genre index are observed in the speeches of Krassikov (59.1 percent) and Vyshinskiy (49.5 percent). A high level of a categorical judgment in the speeches for the prosecution is explained by the fact that these state prosecutors had to play at the trials as well as an actor acts out the play, and this fact is confirmed by the mechanical speech behaviour of Krassikov and Vyshinskiy. A frequent use of the speech signals on the plane of certain statement by these state prosecutors is vivid proof that, in the example of Vyshinskiy, the prosecutors' body was a tool of punishment, as well as security. Vyshinskiy in his time put forward a terrible theory: "The avowal of guilt is the queen of all proofs," and everybody knows how these evidences of all the arrested were "beaten out" (Beria, n.d.). Therefore, pleasing the authorities' so-called "strong belief" is based more on the famous theory of presumption of guilt. This assumption is also proved by a high rate of negative attitude to a speech event (see below), indicating pessimism of these authors. Self-confident people are generally cheerful and optimistic.

Less commonly, the speech signals of the plane of certain statement are actualised in the speeches for the prosecution made by Pokrovskiy (29.2 percent) and Koni (33.3 percent) compared with the average speech-genre index of 43.5 percent. It indicates a low confidence level of their speech behaviour. These public prosecutors are not categorical in their opinions because of their shyness and hesitation, and have no such quality as courage. These people are prisoners of constant doubt, and are highly selective and cautious in the contacts (Kunitsyna, Kazarinova and Pogolsha 2002, 426). Very often, unsure people have a low self-esteem and they often tend to reproach themselves and are sensitive to any criticism (Enikeev 2002, 491).

The implicit speech strategy "The sender's formation of addressee's attitude to a speech event by evaluation"

As is shown by the material of our study, the average speech-genre index of the plane of forming the addressee's positive attitude to a speech event by evaluation has significantly lower rates (14.3 percent) than the rates of forming the negative attitude (49.8 percent). Let us take the latter into account with the fact that the negative attitude prevails in the court speeches for the prosecution of all the addressers.

Most often, the markers of the plane of forming the addressee's negative attitude to a speech event by evaluation are used by Vyshinskiy (64.8 percent) and Pokrovskiy (57.4 percent) with the already high average speech-genre index at 49.8 percent. The speech behaviour of the public prosecutors of that time reflects the realities of the trial system in the

1920s to 1940s, when the accusatory court tendency was manifested in an automatic, mechanical speech behaviour of the public prosecutors.

As already mentioned, in his speeches Vyshinskiy's emphasis had to be not on the evidence, mainly because the verdict was already a foregone conclusion, but on rhetoric and pathos. This is not because "The Chief Inquisitor" Vyshinskiy was a bad lawyer, it was because it was necessary not so much to justify an established process but to prepare the ground for a future one (Zvyagintsev 2001, 82). Additionally, such speeches were full of coarse, insulting statements, called "invectives."

From a psychological point of view, the high indices of negative attitude tell us about the pessimism of the above-mentioned speakers. In Vyshinskiy's speeches, the same is conferred by the low level of the plane of personal participation and the high percentage of the plane of objective participation of the implicit speech strategy "Participation/ Nonparticipation of members of communication in a speech event" (see above). Moreover, contemporary reports show that Vyshinskiy delivered his speeches at the court emotionally and with a great passion (Zvyagintsev 2001, 80), and it is also shown by the lowest neutral evaluation (19 percent compared to the average speech-genre index of 35.9 percent).

An even greater pessimist is Pokrovskiy, in whose speeches we see a combination of a high negative attitude to a speech event at 57.4 percent (the average speech-genre index is 49.8 percent), a low positive evaluation of 9.1 percent of the implicit studied strategy (the average speech-genre index is 14.3 percent), a low level of certain statement at 29.2 percent of the implicit speech strategy "Sure/Unsure speech behaviour of an author" (the average speech-genre index is 43.5 percent), and a low index of the plane of personal participation at 4.5 percent of the implicit speech strategy "Participation/Nonparticipation of members of communication in a speech event" (the average speech-genre index is 10 percent).

All things considered, none of the seven public prosecutors during the 1920s to 1940s, whose judicial speeches we have studied, is an optimist by nature, as the indicators of the negative evaluation are significantly higher than those of the positive attitude. Considering the average speech-genre index of forming a positive attitude to a speech event by evaluation at 14.3 percent, more often we find the markers of this plane in the court speeches of Koni (21 percent) and Lunacharskiy (18 percent). These authors are trying to arouse positive emotions in their listeners, or at least have the minimum psychological intention of raising positive emotions of addressees in the face of global condemnation, reflecting not only the optimistic mood of these public prosecutors but also a certain humanity.

Thus, we have analysed the individual speech behaviour of the public prosecutors of the USSR in the 1920s to 1940s and have diagnosed some individual personal qualities of these prosecutors.

2.3. Russian-speaking prosecutors' speech behaviour at the beginning of the twenty-first century

2.3.1. Russian-speaking prosecutors' speech behaviour at the beginning of the twenty-first century before a professional trial

The texts of the speeches for the prosecution of Russian-speaking public prosecutors at the beginning of the twenty-first century before a professional trial were divided into 5,377 MSGs, as shown in table 4 (see appendix). Let us study the data of this table.

The implicit speech strategy "Participation/Nonparticipation of members of communication in a speech event"

The average speech-genre index of the plane of personal participation is 31.2 percent. The highest rates of this plane are found in the speeches of Shinkarov (44.6 percent) and Baev (43.4 percent). It indicates the fact that the state prosecutors consider their own point of view to be of great importance. These indices, combined with the lowest level of the plane of objective participation (Shinkarov has 54.3 percent and Baev 55.2 percent, compared with the average of 68.1 percent) indicate that these state prosecutors are extroverts.

Based on the studies of psychological literature one can make a general portrait of an extrovert. As a rule, it is an impulsive person who easily gives way, but is sometimes unreasonably stubborn and cocky. They are always in motion, are playful, superficial, vain, lacking self-control, expansive and have a tendency to exaggerate. Such a person is inclined to public speaking, easily make friends and comrades, and cannot stand loneliness (Kunitsyna, Kazarinova and Pogolsha 2002, 426–427). Perhaps Shinkarov and Baev possess the above-mentioned individual personal qualities.

The lowest indices of the plane of personal participation are in the speeches for the prosecution of Kondakov (2.7 percent) and Glyuzitskiy (22.6 percent). These authors are not leaders by nature, are modest and do not over-emphasise their ego or "self." It is possible that this factor is connected to the fear of expressing their own point of view (especially considering the indices of the implicit speech strategy "Sure/Unsure speech behaviour of an author," see below).

The average speech-genre index of the plane of social participation is 0.7 percent. The level of this plane is extremely low, so we cannot speak about the special communication skills of any public prosecutors whose speeches are now being studied. We would like to note that some public prosecutors (Agapov, Fedorin and Makhno) do not actualise these speech signals of the plane of social participation at all, their index being at zero. They are pushing for the plane of personal participation. Generally speaking, the cooperative type of behaviour is not their distinctive feature. Most likely, these authors have a high self-esteem and a tendency for self-admiration, or they just do not possess the skill of public speaking.

Now let us study the data of the plane of objective participation. The highest indices of this plane are observed in the speeches for the prosecution of Kondakov (95.7 percent) and Glyuzitskiy (76.8 percent), whereas the average is 68.1 percent. Actualising the signals of the plane of objective participation more often than others, these public prosecutors automatically affect the addressee with the help of the objective picturing of reality, as much as possible. The behaviour of the public prosecutors with high rates of the plane of objective participation of the implicit speech strategy "Participation/Nonparticipation of members of communication in a speech event" has an orientation to the inner life and self-analysis, because these state prosecutors are introverts.

The implicit speech strategy "Sure/Unsure speech behaviour of an author"

The average speech-genre index of the plane of certain statement is 56.1 percent. The most determined and confident people are public prosecutors Shinkarov and Baev, whose levels of the categorical statement are 78.9 percent and 69.7 percent respectively. They have the energy and perseverance to persuade judges. People with high levels of the categorical statement like Shinkarov and Baev are able to express their views freely. They openly talk about their thoughts and often use the personal pronoun "I." They are not afraid of expressing their own opinion (let us also remember the highest rates of the plane of personal participation of the implicit speech strategy "Participation/Nonparticipation of members of communication in a speech event").

The state prosecutors in whose speeches the signals of uncertain statement dominate are careful in their speech behaviour. That is why we can say that they are irresolute and not always sure of their strength. The average speech-genre index of the uncertain statement is 43.9 percent. The highest rates are seen in the speeches for the prosecution of A. Kondakov (73.6 percent) and Glyuzitskiy (50.3 percent). This data, along with the low rates of the plane of personal participation (see above) show that Kondakov and Glyuzitskiy unconsciously avoid responsibility and have some individual personal qualities connected to uncertain behaviour.

The implicit speech strategy "The sender's formation of addressee's attitude to a speech event by evaluation"

According to the results of our study this group of public prosecutors, as well as the previous groups, is characterised by the predominance of negative attitude. However, even among this group one can select those who have the most expressed pessimism. Thus, the highest rates of the plane of negative attitude show the strongly pronounced pessimism of Glyuzitskiy (64.7 percent) and Baev (64.1 percent), compared with the average speech-genre index 58.1 percent. We can say that from the very beginning these public prosecutors are receptive only to a negative perception of the world rather than a positive one.

The average speech-genre index of the plane of positive attitude is 11.8 percent, which is certainly below the average speech-genre index of the plane of negative attitude (58.1 percent). However, we can say that the public prosecutors with the indicators which are above the average speech-genre index of the plane of positive attitude (11.8 percent) are less pessimistic, of course, as far as it is possible. They are more philosophical about life as a whole and about a committed crime in particular. They more often pay attention to positive aspects. These public prosecutors are Agapov (18 percent of the plane of positive attitude) and Fedorin (16.7 percent of the plane of positive attitude).

A high index of evaluation generally indicates the spontaneity and frankness of a person, but also it often shows their irresponsibility and impulsiveness (Stepanov 2003, 305–306). We can find the confirmation of this position is the following fact: the lowest indices of neutral evaluation of a speech event of the prosecutors studied (19.3 percent of Baev and 21.7 percent of Shinkarov, whereas the average speech-genre index is 30.1 percent) correlate with the highest rates of certain statement (see above).

However, a low index of the evaluation proves a person to be unemotional. Among such individuals we can see Kondakov, who has the highest neutral evaluation of the situation (39 percent compared to the average 30.1 percent).

We have diagnosed some personal qualities of the representatives of Russian-speaking public prosecutors before a professional trial at the beginning of the twenty-first century through studying their speech behaviour. Now let us analyse the speech behaviour of a similar group of prosecutors speaking in court but before another addressee—a trial by jury.

2.3.2. Russian-speaking prosecutors' speech behaviour at the beginning of the twenty-first century before a trial by jury

The speeches of Russian-speaking prosecutors at the beginning of the twenty-first century before a trial by jury were divided into 2,917 MSGs, recorded in table 5 (see appendix). Now we will study the speech behaviour of public prosecutors basing on data from the table.

The implicit speech strategy "Participation/Nonparticipation of members of communication in a speech event"

The average speech-genre index of the plane of personal participation is 18.1 percent. The difference to the bigger degree is observed in the speeches for the prosecution of Trukhanov (22.7 percent), Fedorov (21.3 percent) and Melnikov (20 percent), indicating that these state prosecutors have a great inclination to independence, dominance and leadership.

The low indices of the plane of personal participation of Salnikov (13.1 percent) and Romanov (13.2 percent) are likely to mean conformity, dependence, shyness and modesty.

Now let us turn to the indicators of the plane of social participation. The average speech-genre index here is 6.7 percent. Above this mark there are the indices of Truhanov (12 percent), Kozyr (7.6 percent) and Abramov (7 percent). In these speeches for the prosecution the authors, who tend to actualise the plane of social participation, unconsciously make their passive listener an active participant of the communication. In terms of the psychological diagnosis, they are friendly and they are able to make successful social interaction.

State prosecutors with low indices of the plane of social participation, by contrast, are formal in contacts with the people around them and even avoid the world. We refer Melnikov (2.3 percent) and Salnikov (3.2 percent) as such people—they are probably inflexible not only in their speech but also their everyday behaviour.

The implicit speech strategy "Sure/Unsure speech behaviour of an author"

The average speech-genre index of the certain statement is 40.6 percent. The high level of the certain statement we see in Fedorov's (58.3 percent) and Truhanov's (48.8 percent) speeches. These people are not afraid to face facts. They infect listeners with their confidence in providing information, and in everyday life they are also constant in their plans and affections.

The indicators below the average speech-genre index are observed in the speeches of Salnikov (19 percent) and Abramov (33.9 percent). It shows that the authors of these speeches avoid responsibility, do not seek to defend their points of view, follow a more powerful person, do not believe in themselves and in their abilities, and so are passive.

The implicit speech strategy "The sender's formation of addressee's attitude to a speech event by evaluation"

Most often in this group of public prosecutors, one can see the plane of negative attitude to a speech event in the speeches of Salnikov and Abramov. Having the average speech-genre index of the plane of negative attitude to a speech event 37.5 percent, their indices are 43.7 percent and 43.3 percent respectively.

In my opinion, the high values of negative attitude demonstrate that these state prosecutors anxious and worry about the future. Salnikov and Abramov are most likely preoccupied by the consequences of their actions, constantly anticipating failure and misfortune. Therefore, their speech behaviour is also uncertain, and is proved by the lowest rates of the certain statement.

Positive attitude is most common in the speeches for the prosecution of Kozyr (14.4 percent) and Abramov (12.1 percent), where the average speech-genre index is 10 percent. We believe that such people are less pessimistic than their colleagues. They are more cheerful, joyful and energetic. Having a higher positive set than the others, it is easier for them to find understanding among their listeners. Therefore, we can also talk about Kozyr's and Abramov's manifestation of a social life, comparing with their highest rates of the plane of social participation.

Having described some personal qualities of the representatives of Russian-speaking public prosecutors at the beginning of the twenty-first century speaking before a trial by jury, we will begin studying the personal qualities of a similar, but English-speaking group of public prosecutors.

3. English-speaking prosecutors' speech behaviour at the beginning of the twenty-first century in speaking before a trial by jury

The texts are divided into 3,196 MSGs and the results are compiled in table 6 (see appendix). Let us study these results.

The implicit speech strategy "Participation/Nonparticipation of members of communication in a speech event"

The average speech-genre index of the plane of personal participation is 13.2 percent. The highest index of this plane belongs to Andrade (22.3 percent). It shows his inclination for leadership, authoritativeness, independence, courage and confidence. He can ignore social conventions, lives by his own laws and actively defends his independence.

The low values of the plane of personal participation in the speeches of Whylie (9.3 percent) and Smith (9.5 percent) indicate the caution of the authors, who are afraid of expressing their individuality and responsibility for what has been said.

As for the plane of social participation, one can see that the average speech-genre index (5.9 percent) is exceeded by the indices of Templeman's (10.8 percent) and Whylie's (10.7 percent) speeches. These prosecutors demonstrate their openness to their interlocutor, involving the latter in a dialogue. They are able to establish and maintain an emotional contact with the participants of communication.

The low levels of the plane of social participation of Smith (2.7 percent) and Dennis (3 percent) may be a signal of some difficulties in the construction of interpersonal communication. They are not always ready to cooperate, and are passive in contact and unsociable.

The implicit speech strategy "Sure/Unsure speech behaviour of an author"

The average speech-genre index of the plane of certain statement is 23.5 percent. Significant deviations from this value to the bigger level are observed in the speeches for the prosecution of Templeman (70.3 percent). These figures tell us about determination, courage and even resistance to the threat.

The indicators which are lower than the average speech-genre index of the plane of certain statement (23.5 percent) are in the speeches of Reid (8.9 percent) and Smith (11.1 percent). Such people are not confident in their abilities and are unreasonably tormented by feelings of worthlessness, and are restrained in manifesting their emotions (not without reason they have the highest rates of the plane of neutral attitude, see below), they do not like working in a team—do not forget that they also have low indices of the plane of social participation: Smith (2.7 percent), and Reid (4.7 percent). The average speech-genre index of the plane of social participation is 5.9 percent.

The implicit speech strategy "The sender's formation of addressee's attitude to a speech event by evaluation"

The average speech-genre index of the plane of negative attitude to a speech event by evaluation in the speeches of the English-speaking public prosecutors before the trial jury is 25.7 percent, twice the average speech-genre index of the plane of positive attitude to a speech event by evaluation (12.5 percent).

Most often the markers of negative evaluation are used by Dennis (33.7 percent) and Andrade (29.2 percent). Therefore, diagnosing their personal qualities one can say that they have a pessimistic assessment of the events being spoken about. Dennis and Andrade are focused on problems and emotional experiences. They are anxious and have a vulnerable self-esteem (which may be also indicated by the highest indices of the plane of personal participation).

The predominance of the plane of positive attitude in comparison with other state prosecutors is characteristic for such English-speaking prosecutors as Templeman (19.4 percent) and Andrade (17.7 percent). The average speech-genre index of the plane of positive attitude, as we have already said, is 12.5 percent.

Templeman and Andrade in comparison with other state prosecutors to some extent demonstrate peace of mind, some kind of serenity of mood and a certain vitality. These prosecutors are less pessimistic people, they are more satisfied with their lives, and therefore may have more faith in success and in their strength.

We have made an attempt to diagnose some of the individual personal traits of public prosecutors in the relatively homogeneous groups of different time periods, speaking in front of different addressees and belonging to different national and cultural groups. Now we will study the stereotyped speech behaviour of the same groups of public prosecutors in general.

PART III

COMPARATIVE ANALYSIS OF *STEREOTYPED* SPEECH BEHAVIOUR OF PROSECUTORS

I would like to begin the study of stereotyped speech behaviour of prosecutors by mentioning that for the analysis there were taken relatively homogeneous speeches for the prosecution. All are connected to criminal cases and all prosecutors are male. The comparison was carried out according to (a) different **periods of history**: the speeches of Russian-speaking public prosecutors in speaking before a trial by jury at the end of the nineteenth century and at the beginning of the twenty-first century, and before a professional trial in the 1920s to 1940s and at the beginning of the twenty-first century; (b) different **addressees**: the speeches of Russian-speaking public prosecutors at the beginning of the twenty-first century in speaking before a trial by jury and before a professional trial; (c) different **lingua-cultural communities:** the speeches of public prosecutors (Russian-speaking and English-speaking) in speaking before a trial by jury at the beginning of the twenty-first century.

The results of the pragmalinguistic experiment are compiled in table 7 (see appendix). We will consider the data of this table according to the three implicit speech strategies: "Participation/Nonparticipation of members of communication in a speech event," "Sure/Unsure speech behaviour of an author," and "The sender's formation of addressee's attitude to a speech event by evaluation."

1. Comparative analysis of stereotyped speech behaviour of Russian-speaking prosecutors in different periods of history

1.1. Comparative analysis of stereotyped speech behaviour of Russian-speaking prosecutors in speaking before a trial by jury in the nineteenth and the twenty-first century

The implicit speech strategy "Participation/Nonparticipation of members of communication in a speech event"

The average speech-genre index of the plane of personal participation is 17.5 percent. In speeches before a trial by jury at the end of the nineteenth century it is 12.4 percent, and at the beginning of the twenty-first century it is 18.1 percent. Such a difference of indicators may be connected to the tasks carried out by prosecutors at various stages of development and with the personal qualities of the public prosecutors at different periods of history.

Regarding the tasks of the prosecutor's office, one can say that at the end of the nineteenth century it served as "a faithful guardian of government's interests" (Rossiyskoe zakonodatelstvo 1991, 30). Historians show that the legal tradition in Russia was weak (Berman 1963). In Tsarist Russia, as in other autocratic states, the sovereign stood above the law (Solomon 1988, 10). A state prosecutor acted not so much on his own behalf but on behalf of the monarch. Therefore, the indices of the plane of personal participation in his speeches are lower than in those of a modern public prosecutor.

Presently, at the beginning of the twenty-first century, a prosecutor acts (or at least should act) in accordance with the principle of independence, which means existing his own competence of the prosecution. No other state bodies, government agencies, local governments, public associations, their representatives and officials or mass media may interfere in the work of the public prosecutor's office (Savyuk 2001, 405). Maybe that is why the indices of the plane of personal participation are higher than the average speech-genre index.

The next factor influencing the plane of personal participation is the difference in personal qualities of Russian public prosecutors in different centuries. Modern state prosecutors have some personal traits which are expressed more clearly in the present day, for example the will and desire for leadership are such signs of our time (Varnavskikh 2002, 270).

The implicit speech strategy "Sure/Unsure speech behaviour of an author"

The average speech-genre index of the plane of certain statement in the speeches of the public prosecutions is 43 percent. As for the speeches of Russian-speaking public prosecutors before a trial by jury in the nineteenth century and in the twenty-first century, we can say that these groups have minimal differences in their stereotyped speech behaviour from the point of view of certainty/uncertainty, as minimal differences in the percentages are demonstrated (42.4 percent and 40.6 percent respectively, whereas the average is 43 percent).

Based on the data of the pragmalinguistic experiment, we cannot talk about big differences in the speech behaviour of the public prosecutors working in the nineteenth century and in the twenty-first century from the point of view of Sure/Unsure speech behaviour of the authors. We can only note that these groups of public prosecutors unconsciously actualise in their speech behaviour the signals of certain statement, close to the average speech-genre index of stereotyped verbal behaviour of the whole group of public prosecutors, and unconsciously follow the unwritten rules of stereotyped speech behaviour of the prosecutors, surely one of the signs of their professionalism.

The implicit speech strategy "The sender's formation of addressee's attitude to a speech event by evaluation"

We can see some differences in the speech behaviour of these groups of public prosecutors in the formation of the addressee's negative attitude towards a crime. The average speech-genre index is 45 percent—in the speeches of the nineteenth century it is 43 percent and in those of the twenty-first century it is 37.5 percent. Perhaps these figures show that now a greater number of public prosecutors are familiar with the basics of psychology regarding the impact of verbal influence, and modern public prosecutors intuitively use a more positive mood of the audience for persuasion when they actualise stereotyped speech behaviour. This spirit is particularly relevant for today's Russia, a non-stable society in a "phase of social transformation" (Rozin 1997, 80). Therefore, the abundance of negative information generates disapproval and rejection.

Comparing the sender's methods of forming the addressee's attitude to a speech event by evaluation, one can see that the indices of the plane of positive attitude in the speeches of public prosecutors of Russia before a trial by jury in the nineteenth century (11 percent) and in the twenty-fist century (10 percent) are close to the average speech-genre index of 12 percent. Therefore, it is impossible to talk about fundamental differences. The public prosecutors of both periods actualise positive attitude, unconsciously following the stereotyped speech behaviour of the public prosecutor as a representative of a certain kind of legal branch.

We will now move on to a comparative speech analysis of Russian-speaking public prosecutors in different periods of history and study their stereotyped speech behaviour before a professional trial in the 1920s to 1940s, and at the beginning of the twenty-first century.

1.2. Comparative analysis of stereotyped speech behaviour of Russian-speaking prosecutors before a professional trial in the 1920s to 1940s and at the beginning of the twenty-first century

The implicit speech strategy "Participation/Nonparticipation of members of communication in a speech event"

According to the results of the pragmalinguistic experiment, the average speech-genre index of the plane of personal participation is 17.5 percent. The level of this plane of prosecution speeches in the 1920s to 1940s is 10 percent, and at the beginning of the twenty-first century it is 31.2 percent. Why is there is a significant difference in the percentages? In my opinion, the speech behaviour of public prosecutors as representatives of the state is inseparable from the time in the life of the country, and to some extent it is a reflection of processes taking place in the society.

In the 1920s to 1940s, every honest person lived with difficulty, and it was especially difficult for those who possessed the qualities which Marx called "objective revolutionary": criticism, courage, integrity and the ability to resist public opinion. Stalin promoted in the Soviet society the opposite, "objective antirevolutionary" human qualities: lying, loyalty to authorities, cowardice of thought and words, corruption and opportunism (Makarenko 1989, 104).

As the historical documents show, a significant amount of forensic prosecutors themselves became victims of repression (Solomon 1988, 226). Very few state prosecutors were able to find the courage and a sincere desire to take such a responsibility themselves. That is why in the stereotyped speech behaviour of public prosecutors before a professional trial in the 1920s to 1940s we see a low actualisation of the plane of personal participation of the implicit speech strategy "Participation/ Nonparticipation of members of communication in a speech event."

Now the situation, of course, is different. In recent years the value orientations of Russian society has changed rapidly. Previously many ethical problems were solved on the basis of the well-known principle: "to be moral is to be useful for the revolution, for the building of communism." Today, when the former inspiring idea has disappeared, and there is a fundamental breakdown of the socio-economic relations, the functions of the state and the direction of its policies are changing, and there is a radical rethinking of the understanding of a social duty and moral responsibility of a person (Pavlova 2001, 104). That is why the level of personal participation of public prosecutors at the beginning of the twenty-first century is so high.

The indices of the plane of social participation are also interesting. Compared with the average speech-genre index, which is 6.9 percent, the plane of social participation in the 1920s to 1940s is the highest at 13.6 percent, whereas at the beginning of the twenty-first century it only reaches the level of 0.7 percent. To my mind, this phenomenon can be explained by the fact that in the era of socialism, when the collective was a priority over the individual, the plane of social participation is actualised more frequently than at present, when personal achievements have the highest value among public prosecutors of the "democratic" society.

The implicit speech strategy "Sure/Unsure speech behaviour of an author"

In accordance with the results of the pragmalinguistic experiment, the average speech-genre index of certain statement is 43 percent. The indices of the speeches before a professional trial in the 1920s to 1940s are nearly equal to this level—43.5 percent. The greatest differences compared with the average speech-genre index are in the speeches for the prosecution at the beginning of the twenty-first century—56.1 percent. Therefore, the difference here is 13.1 percent.

Modern public prosecutors, in proving a crime and that the defendant is guilty, must be sure of the information provided to the court, otherwise they are obliged to abandon their incrimination. The ability to change their own conclusions suggests the presence of such qualities in prosecutors as self-criticism, self-control, and seeking the truth even if connected to admission of their own error (Kravchenko, n.d.). In this regard, we observe a high percentage of the certain statement in the speech behaviour of the modern state prosecutors in the speeches before professional judges.

The implicit speech strategy "The sender's formation of addressee's attitude to a speech event by evaluation"

Based on the analysis data, one can note that the average speech-genre index of formation of a positive attitude to a speech event is 12 percent. In the speeches of Russian-speaking public prosecutors before a professional tribunal in the 1920s to 1940s the index is 14.3 percent, and at the beginning of the twenty-first century it is 11.8 percent.

It should be noted that the rate of a positive attitude in the 1920s to 1940s is the highest among all the groups of the state prosecutors. Perhaps this fact is explained by the specific ideology of the time when everyone lived in expectation of a brighter future and the building of communism, as there is one thing to be noted: all the examples of a positive attitude do not relate to the wrongful act, the accused or the victim, but to praising the role of the Party and the Government in Soviet society.

The negative attitude is actualised in 49.8 percent of speeches made in the 1920s to 1940s and in 58.15 percent of cases from the beginning of the twenty-first century. The average speech-genre index is 45 percent. The high rates of public prosecutors' formation of a negative attitude to a wrongful act in the Soviet period is due to the fact that this was a time of profound social conflicts, of undeclared war with its people, the so-called "class" (political) struggle, and "class" enemies. The society was accustomed to act according to a simple idea, that the main purpose is to seek the guilty, to find and to punish enemies, but moreover it is best to destroy them (Vitsin 1999, 11). All of these processes, of course, found reflection in the formation of public consciousness of the people in general, and public prosecutors in particular.

In the Soviet era, there was such an effective system of propaganda that until now, despite dramatic changes in the society, many of those who are entrusted with power are in thrall to the lessons studied during this period (Koshelyuk, n.d.). We see the confirmation of this fact in the using of a negative attitude by the modern state prosecutors speaking before professional judges (as opposed to the speeches for the prosecution before the jury as shown below).

There is a cruelty to some prosecutors now which is impossible to explain, but the brutality and bloodlust is the sad legacy of Vishinsky, rather than the tradition of pre-revolutionary Russian prosecutors. Progressive lawyers have been always been guided by the commandment of the Moscow Metropolitan Filaret, that even if a crime is disgraceful, a person is worthy of pity (Kucherena, n.d.).

We can see a clear presence of the stereotyped extremes in the speech behaviour of the Russian-speaking public prosecutors at the beginning of the twenty-first century speaking before a professional trial, which are expressed in the tendency to accusation.

Therefore, in the course of the pragmalinguistic experiment we found that stereotyped speech behaviour of the public prosecutors is directly dependent on the time frame, that is on a historic period. All things considered, there are differences in the stereotyped speech behaviour of the Russian-speaking public prosecutors before a trial by jury in the nineteenth century and in the twenty-first century, as before a professional trial in the 1920s to 1940s and at the beginning of the twenty-first century.

In the next section we will analyse whether there are any differences in stereotyped speech behaviour of the Russian-speaking public prosecutors of the same period (the beginning of the twenty-first century), before both a professional trial and a trial by jury.

2. Comparative analysis of stereotyped speech behaviour of Russian-speaking prosecutors before different addressees

Let us now study speeches for the prosecution of Russian-speaking public prosecutors before different addressees (a professional trial and a trial by jury) at the beginning of the twenty-first century. We will seek to find whether or not any speech by its very nature has a dialogic character, as projected onto another person, their understanding and their actual or possible answer (Agapova 2002, 14), or whether it depends on the definite addressee.

The implicit speech strategy "Participation/Nonparticipation of members of communication in a speech event"

As shown by the research material, the average speech-genre index of the plane of personal participation is 17.5 percent, in the speeches before professional judges it is equal to 31.2 percent and before a trial by jury it is 18.1 percent. In our opinion, the frequent actualisation of the plane of personal participation before a professional trial is due to the following factors.

Firstly, for a public prosecutor it is to make understandable their own point of view. The most important thing for them is proving their own position concerning the main points and the details of the crime, the position of a public prosecutor.

Secondly, speaking before a professional trial a public prosecutor addresses primarily to the court, which consists of one person (the judge) and, therefore, the speech behaviour of a public prosecutor is mainly directed to the personality of the judge. Speaking to the professional judge, a prosecutor does not practically actualise the inclusive "we," as the linguistic intuition of a public prosecutor tells them that it may cause a negative reaction from the judge, accustomed to independence and the formation of their own point of view without the interference of anyone else. The speech behaviour is automatically adjusted to the specific addressee.

The level of the plane of social participation in the court speeches before professional judges is 0.7 percent, but before a trial by jury it is 6.7 percent—almost the same as the average speech-genre index which is 6.9 percent. In the speeches for the court of jurors, the prosecutor's intuition tells them that it is not enough just to demonstrate his position in all the details, actualising the plane of personal participation of the implicit speech strategy "Participation/Nonparticipation of members of communication in a speech event." Experience shows that the jurors often do not have any trial practice and do not realise not only the details of the proceedings, but also that they cannot understand even the essence of the case. The representatives of this type of trial are intuitively happy to be helped, especially because they do not have an opportunity to participate directly, to ask questions, and are involved only by using their "ears."

Here, an experienced public prosecutor, actualising the plane of social participation of the implicit speech strategy "Participation/ Nonparticipation of members of communication in a speech event," unconsciously extends a helping hand to the jury. Moreover, a public prosecutor as a representative of the state and the law is to inspire confidence and solidarity of the trial by jurors as a priority. This is not an easy task, as opinion polls clearly show that the level of trust—and this is one of the key parameters in the relationship "power/people"—is extremely low (Pocheptsov 2001, 252). In such a situation, when people do not believe law enforcement agencies and authorities, the cooperative type of behaviour of a public prosecutor is a good means of implicit speech influence on the jurors.

The implicit speech strategy "Sure/Unsure speech behaviour of an author"

According to the results of the pragmalinguistic experiment, the highest indices of certain statement are typical for the prosecutors' speeches before professional judges—56.1 percent. Before the jurors, this figure is much lower at 40.6 percent. The average speech-genre index is 43 percent. As one can see, the speeches for a professional trial are characterised by a pronounced certainty.

In such speeches, the influence on others is generated because of self-confidence, which comes from the sureness of oneself, one's own presentation and the surrounding. The high categorical behaviour in the speeches before the professional judges indicates that in this type of procedure it is still valid the division between "insiders" and "outsiders" which was characteristic for the period of building socialism in the USSR. "Insiders" should be taught, persuaded and re-persuaded, and "outsiders" should be unmasked and destroyed (this fact is also proved by the highest negative evaluation, see below). Sometimes, speeches characterised by higher sure behaviour can only increase the "protest" mood among the audience (Chaika, n.d.). The public prosecutors speaking for a trial by jury somehow feel it and unconsciously actualise the lower level of certain statement, which, in turn, causes much less antagonism of a trial by jury.

The implicit speech strategy "The sender's formation of addressee's attitude to a speech event by evaluation"

The indicators of forming a positive attitude to a speech event by evaluation in the speeches for the prosecution before a professional trial (11.8 percent) and before a trial by jury (10 percent) are close to the average speech-genre index of 12 percent. That is why there is no sense in talking about any specific differences in their speech behaviour according to this parameter.

Let us turn to the plane of forming a negative attitude to a speech event by evaluation. The average speech-genre index here is 45 percent. In the speeches before professional judges it is 58.1 percent, and in front of a trial by jury it is 37.5 percent.

In the speech behaviour before a trial of professionals we are seeing a clear trend towards the accusation. This factor is associated with three major "defects or mortal sins" (Kucherena, n.d.) of a modern public prosecutor's office. They are: accusatory trend, permissiveness and inexplicable cruelty.

Thus, the results of the pragmalinguistic experiment show that the stereotyped speech behaviour with respect to the similar groups of public prosecutors who are speaking the same language (Russian) and belong to the similar time period (the beginning of the twenty-first century) has significant differences in the presentation to different addressees: a professional trial or a trial by jury.

In the next experiment we will compare stereotyped speech behaviour of the groups of public prosecutors working at the same period before a trial by jury, but having different national and cultural characteristics, in this case the Russian and English languages.

3. Comparative analysis of stereotyped speech behaviour of prosecutors belonging to different lingua-cultural communities (Russian-speaking and English-speaking)

The speeches of Russian-speaking and English-speaking public prosecutors working at the beginning of the twenty-first century before a trial by jury are analysed here. The results are recorded in table 7 (see appendix). Let us compare the stereotyped speech behaviour of the public prosecutors of Russia and the UK.

The implicit speech strategy "Participation/Nonparticipation of members of communication in a speech event"

According to the results of the pragmalinguistic experiment, we estimated that the average speech-genre index of the plane of personal participation is 17.5 percent. In the speeches before the Russian jury, the level of this plane is 18.1 percent, whereas before the British jury it is 13.2 percent.

Russian-speaking addressers actualise the plane of personal participation of the implicit speech strategy "Participation/ Nonparticipation of members of communication in a speech event" more often, showing a tendency towards an authoritarian type of verbal behaviour. For the Russian communicative consciousness, it is inherent in a purely peculiar national idea of limited communicative sovereignty of a personality: the Russian consciousness considers acceptable a communicative invasion of privacy. Moreover, it can be almost any person and it can happen in almost any conditions.

The Russian existential consciousness sees no obstacles in speaking to anyone. One can make comments to strangers, give them advice, and it is possible to interfere in the conversation of people, to ask one of them a question. One can "hang" one's own problems on others, request a favour of strangers, can express an opinion about the fact that is being discussed by a number of strangers, can correct them, explain their errors, and it is possible to approach any person closely, to touch an interlocutor, and so on (Sternin, n.d.).

However, the English speakers as state prosecutors are less focused on personality. For the Western communicative consciousness, the categories of communicative integrity and tolerance are much more expressed, and the categories of politeness and communicative ideal are based on the concept of privacy or "personal integrity" (Sternin, n.d.). An English-speaking addresser is characterised by a specific characteristic such as adherence to the "ideology of correctness" (Aseeva 1999, 5).

During the pragmalinguistic experiment we found that the actualisations of the plane of social participation of the implicit speech strategy "Participation/Nonparticipation of members of communication in a speech event" in the speeches of the Russian public prosecutors (6.7 percent) and in the speeches of the British public prosecutors (5.9 percent) in general are the same, and do not significantly differ from the average speech-genre index of 6.9 percent.

With all the differences in the levels of socio-economic and cultural development, in special traits of the legal systems and mechanisms for justice in one or another country, the determinants and the nature of a public opinion are much more general than specific. All studies confirm that legal ignorance, incomplete and distorted legal views are considered to be a universal factor (Kvashis 1997, 56), and it also applies to a group of jurors.

The law is a rather vague category not only for Russia. The same thing can be said about the British jury, as the processes of democratisation in the British legal system also touched this institution: in 1972 a property limit was abolished and the age limit for jurors was lowered (Istoria 1998, 577).

Jurors cannot understand all the detailed circumstances of a criminal case, and moreover they do not need to understand the specific rules, the pros and cons, of the law. They are more likely to rely on their own experience. However, a public prosecutor is a professional lawyer, and to bridge the gap between his own professionalism and inexperience in legal cases of the jurors both Russian-speaking and English-speaking public prosecutors will have to become an "insider" for the jurors not to make them dislike and, as a consequence, to reject the position of the public prosecutor. That is why the Russian state prosecutors more often actualise the cooperative type of speech behaviour, unconsciously, and on an existential level they take into account Russian mentality and traditions: a "legal nihilism" established in Russia long ago (Orlov 1999, 63), it is a process when people have a distrust for the law, police, the court and Prosecutor's Office.

Actualising the plane of social participation, that is the cooperative type of speech behaviour, a professional public prosecutor can seek support from a friendly trial by jury, that on an unconscious level begin to understand that the public prosecutor is at least close to them in beliefs and life experience, and is the first step in beginning to trust a public prosecutor.

The implicit speech strategy "Sure/Unsure speech behaviour of an author"

As is shown by the material of our study, the average speech-genre index of the plane of certain statement is 43 percent. The index of certain statement in the speeches before a trial by jury in Russia is a little lower at 40.6 percent. In our opinion, a Russian-speaking public prosecutor takes a clear stance on a committed crime. One can say that his speech behaviour is definite and relatively confident, especially when compared to the verbal behaviour of an English-speaking public prosecutor.

We observe the most significant differences compared with the average speech-genre index (43 percent) in the speech behaviour of the British public prosecutors, which is the lowest among all the studied groups of public prosecutors, their plane of certain statement of an implicit speech strategy "Sure/Unsure speech behaviour of an author" being only 23.5 percent.

High certainty of speech is not a peculiar feature of English-speaking public prosecutors, because it is perceived as disturbing a personal communicative privacy, unacceptable for the British. Extra sureness for English-speaking communicants can even be associated with such a concept as an "argument," which is mostly negative in its evaluation and can even be regarded as a manifestation of aggression (Sternin, n.d.). Therefore, a more certain speech behaviour of the public prosecutors before the English-speaking jurors would not cause the achievement of the goals of persuasion, or as speech experts say, it would be "communicative suicide" (Sternin, n.d.).

The implicit speech strategy "The sender's formation of addressee's attitude to a speech event by evaluation"

According to the results of the pragmalinguistic experiment, we can conclude that the average speech-genre index of the sender's formation of addressee's positive attitude to a speech event by evaluation is 12 percent. This figure is almost equal to that of forming a positive attitude to a speech event by the English-speaking public prosecutors which is 12.5 percent.

The role of a public prosecutor in the UK is not just to participate in the dispute between the state on the one hand and the accused on the other, but in providing to a trial by jury all the information on the case: both favourable and unfavourable to the accused (Sutherland, n.d.).

Perhaps the more optimistic mood of the English-speaking public prosecutors depends on the socio-economic situation in the UK, which is relatively calm and where life is of high quality. Unfortunately, the same cannot be said of Russia.

The index of positive evaluation in the speeches of the Russian-speaking public prosecutors is the lowest at 10 percent. In my opinion, it greatly depends on the socio-political situation. The lower positive intentions of the Russians and the tendency to pessimism are the result of a long difficult situation in the country when the first half of the twentieth century was marked by horrific wars and the second by expectation of war, perhaps even worse for the mental health of the nation. Undoubtedly, all these factors found reflection in the speech behaviour of the Russian-speaking communicants.

Further proof to these words are indicators of the formation of a negative attitude to a speech event by the English-speaking public prosecutors. Despite the fact that the negative evaluation of the Russian-speaking (37.5 percent) and English-speaking (25.7 percent) public prosecutors is lower than the average speech-genre index (45 percent), there is a predominance of accusatory character in a Russian trial by jury.

Therefore, we can conclude that stereotyped speech behaviour differs due to belonging to different lingua-cultural communities.

CONCLUSION

Public prosecutor's behaviour in a speech genre of the speech for the prosecution differs by stylistic originality. This peculiarity refers at the same time to two styles of a literary language, publicistic and official, and secondly, the features of other styles of a literary language: the scientific and colloquial.

However, the features of these styles are unevenly distributed in the speeches of the public prosecutors: the signs of the publicistic style dominate in the prosecution speeches before a trial by jury in the nineteenth and twenty-first centuries in Russia, in the speeches by the English-speaking prosecutors before a trial by jury at the beginning of the twenty-first century and in the speeches of the Russian-speaking prosecutors before a professional trial in the 1920s to 1940s; the signs of the official style dominate in the speeches for the prosecution of the Russian-speaking prosecutors before a professional trial at the beginning of the twenty-first century.

At all times, as an important means of expression, human speech possesses a considerable psycho-diagnosing potential. Human speech can reveal many interesting things about a person. Data obtained through the pragmalinguistic experiment proves this position, coinciding with the characteristics of the public prosecutors, based on the memoirs of their contemporaries and on the results of psycho-diagnostic methods.

Most of the representatives of the professional group of public prosecutors have such individual personal qualities as initiative, self-confidence, concentration on the objective side of things, and the ability to cooperate and to communicate with people. However, at the same time, in the speech behaviour of the state prosecutors there is a tendency to express overconfidence and a pronounced pessimistic attitude towards life. The frequent actualisation of these individual personal qualities is a consequence of the specific nature of public prosecutor's professional duties.

Stereotyped verbal behaviour of the group of public prosecutors was examined with the help of comparative analysis, taking into account the time periods (the end of the nineteenth century, the 1920s to 1940s and the beginning of the twenty-first century), addressees (professional court and trial by the jury), and national-cultural specificity of the addressers

(Russian-speaking and English-speaking public prosecutors). All things considered, we came to the conclusion that:

- speech behaviour of the Russian-speaking public prosecutors before the jury of the twenty-first century differs from the speech behaviour of the similar group of the nineteenth century in a more pronounced tendency to leadership and in less negative attitude.
- speech behaviour of the Russian-speaking public prosecutors before a professional tribunal in the 1920s to 1940s, in contrast to the speech behaviour of the similar group of public prosecutors working at the beginning of the twenty-first century, is characterised by lower actualisation of the plane of personal participation in a speech event, and higher actualisation of the plane of social participation of the implicit speech strategy "Participation/Nonparticipation of members of communication in a speech event." Modern public prosecutors differ in categorical speech behaviour and in the high index of the formation of addressee's negative attitude to a speech event by evaluation.
- speech behaviour of the Russian-speaking public prosecutors of the twenty-first century before a professional trial differs from the similar group of public prosecutors speaking before a trial by the jury through more frequent actualisation of the personal participation in a speech event, in the absence of cooperative behaviour, in the high index of categorical speech behaviour and in the high index of the formation of addressee's negative attitude to a speech event by evaluation;
- speech behaviour of the English-speaking public prosecutors of the twenty-first century before a trial by the jury differs from the similar group of the Russian-speaking public prosecutors through less actualisation of the plane of social participation in a speech event, in significantly lower indices of categorical speech behaviour and in less formation of addressee's negative attitude to a speech event by evaluation.

APPENDIX

Table 1: Fragments of speech behaviour of Russian-speaking public prosecutor Trukhanov in different speech genres

strategies / speech genre	Participation/Nonparticipation of members of communication in a speech event						Sure/Unsure speech behaviour of an author				The sender's formation of addressee's attitude to a speech event by evaluation						MSG
	the plane of **personal** participation		the plane of **social** participation		the plane of **objective** participation		**certain** statement		**uncertain** statement		the plane of **positive** attitude		the plane of **neutral** attitude		the plane of **negative** attitude		
	MSG	%	MSG	%	MSG	%	MSG	%	MSG	%	MSG	%	MSG	%	MSG	%	
1. a speech for a trial by jury	165	22.7	88	12	478	65.3	357	48.8	374	51.2	69	9.4	420	57.5	242	33.1	731
2. a speech for a professional trial	17	7.4	0	0	213	92.6	52	22.6	178	77.4	8	3.5	109	47.4	113	49.1	230

3. a newspaper article	15	5.9	4	1.6	234	92.5	71	28	182	72	29	11.5	110	43.5	114	45	253
4. the average index	197	16.2	92	7.6	925	76.2	480	39.5	734	60.5	106	8.7	639	52.7	469	38.6	1,214
5. *		18.1		6.7		75.2		40.6		59.4		10		52.5		37.5	

* the average speech-genre index of the group of Russian-speaking public prosecutors for a trial by jury in the XXI century

Table 2: Speech behaviour of the group of Russian-speaking public prosecutors for the jury at the end of the nineteenth century

strate-gy / addressers	Participation/Nonparticipation of members of communication in a speech event						Sure/Unsure speech behaviour of an author				The sender's formation of addressee's attitude to a speech event by evaluation						MSG
	the plane of **personal** participation		the plane of **social** participation		the plane of **objective** participation		**certain** statement		**uncertain** statement		the plane of **positive** attitude		the plane of **neutral** attitude		the plane of **negative** attitude		
	MSG	%	MSG	%	MSG	%	MSG	%	MSG	%	MSG	%	MSG	%	MSG	%	
1. Zhukov N. A.	82	8.2	70	7	848	84.8	435	43.5	565	56.5	117	11.7	547	54.7	336	33.6	1,000
2. Koni A. F.	72	7.2	65	6.5	863	86.3	342	34.2	658	65.8	148	14.8	350	35	502	50.2	1,000
3. Plevako F. N.	105	10.5	60	6	835	83.5	414	41.4	586	58.6	99	9.9	457	45.7	444	44.4	1,000
4. Urussov A. I.	138	17	48	6	623	77	284	35.1	525	64.9	82	10.1	443	54.8	284	35.1	809
5. Kazarinov M. G.	56	20.4	19	7	199	72.6	114	41.6	160	58.4	54	21.9	82	29.9	138	55.9	274

6. Muraviov N. V.	55	13	51	12	322	75	240	56	188	44	23	5.4	180	42	225	52.6	428
7. Kessel K. I.	116	24	71	14.7	296	61.3	290	60	193	40	24	5	239	49.5	220	45.5	483
the average speech-genre index	624	12.4	384	7.6	3,986	80	1,185	40.6	1,732	59.4	547	11	2,298	46	2,149	43	4,994

Table 3: Speech behaviour of the group of Russian-speaking public prosecutors in the USSR in the 1900s to 1940s before a professional trial

strategy / addressers	Participation/Nonparticipation of members of communication in a speech event						Sure/Unsure speech behaviour of an author				The sender's formation of addressee's attitude to a speech event by evaluation						MSG
	the plane of **personal** participation		the plane of **social** participation		the plane of **objective** participation		**certain** statement		**uncertain** statement		the plane of **positive** attitude		the plane of **neutral** attitude		the plane of **negative** attitude		
	MSG	%	MSG	%	MSG	%	MSG	%	MSG	%	MSG	%	MSG	%	MSG	%	
1. Krassikov P. A.	52	9.7	159	29.7	325	60.6	317	59.1	219	40.9	71	13.2	183	34.2	282	52.6	536
2. Lunacharskiy A. V.	20	2.5	162	20	628	77.5	284	35	526	65	146	18	262	32.4	402	49.6	810
3. Kon F. N.	166	22.1	86	11.5	498	66.4	250	33.3	500	66.7	158	21	335	44.7	257	34.3	750
4. Kondrushkin I. S.	43	6.8	44	6.9	549	86.3	306	48.1	330	51.9	47	7.4	357	56.1	232	36.5	636
5. Vyshinskiy A. J.	56	5.6	79	7.9	865	86.5	495	49.5	505	50.5	162	16.2	190	19	648	64.8	1,000
6. Krylenko N. V.	132	17	98	12.6	547	70.4	351	45.2	426	54.8	74	9.5	301	38.8	402	51.7	777

7. Pokrovskiy M. N.	13	4.5	24	8.5	247	87	83	29.2	201	70.8	26	9.1	95	33.5	163	57.4	284
the average speech-genre index	482	10	652	13.6	3,659	76.4	2,086	43.5	2,707	56.5	684	14.3	1,723	35.9	2,386	49.8	4,793

Table 4: Speech behaviour of the group of Russian-speaking public prosecutors at the beginning of the twenty-first century before a professional trial

strategy / addressers	Participation/Nonparticipation of members of communication in a speech event						Sure/Unsure speech behaviour of an author				The sender's formation of addressee's attitude to a speech event by evaluation						MSG
	the plane of **personal** participation		the plane of **social** participation		the plane of **objective** participation		**certain** statement		**uncertain** statement		the plane of **positive** attitude		the plane of **neutral** attitude		the plane of **negative** attitude		
	MSG	%	MSG	%	MSG	%	MSG	%	MSG	%	MSG	%	MSG	%	MSG	%	
1. Kondakov A.	25	2.7	14	1.6	873	95.7	241	26.4	671	73.6	60	6.6	356	39	496	54.4	912
2. Glyuzitskiy A.V.	205	22.6	5	0.6	695	76.8	450	49.7	455	50.3	30	3.3	290	32	585	64.7	905
3. Agapov R. V.	285	38	0	0	465	62	450	60	300	40	135	18	285	38	330	44	750
4. Baev V. N.	315	43.4	10	1.4	400	55.2	505	69.7	220	30.3	120	16.6	140	19.3	465	64.1	725

5. Fedorin I. V.	135	30	0	0	315	70	225	50	225	50	75	16.7	150	33.3	225	30	450
6. Shinkarov K. V.	390	44.6	10	1.1	475	54.3	690	78.9	185	21.1	135	15.4	190	21.7	550	62.9	875
7. Makhno N. V.	323	42.5	0	0	437	57.5	456	60	304	40	76	10	209	27.5	475	62.5	760
the average speech-genre index	1,678	31.2	39	0.7	3,660	68.1	3,017	56.1	2,360	43.9	631	11.8	1,620	30.1	3,126	58.1	5,377

Table 5: Speech behaviour of the group of Russian-speaking public prosecutors at the beginning of the twenty-first century before a trial by jury

strategy / addressers	Participation/Nonparticipation of members of communication in a speech event						Sure/Unsure speech behaviour of an author				The sender's formation of addressee's attitude to a speech event by evaluation						MSG
	the plane of **personal** participation		the plane of **social** participation		the plane of **objective** participation		**certain** statement		**uncertain** statement		the plane of **positive** attitude		the plane of **neutral** attitude		the plane of **negative** attitude		
	MSG	%	MSG	%	MSG	%	MSG	%	MSG	%	MSG	%	MSG	%	MSG	%	
1. Trukhanov G. V.	165	22.7	88	12	478	65.3	357	48.8	374	51.2	69	9.4	420	57.5	242	33.1	731
2. Abramov N. V.	72	16.5	31	7	334	76.5	148	33.9	289	66.1	53	12.1	195	44.6	189	43.3	437
3. Salnikov V. N.	49	13.1	12	3.2	312	83.7	71	19	302	81	32	8.6	178	47.7	163	43.7	373
4. Romanov V. I.	49	13.2	17	4.6	306	82.2	132	35.5	240	64.5	23	6.2	223	59.9	126	33.9	372

5. Melnikov A. V.	60	20	7	2.3	233	77.7	125	41.7	175	58.3	33	11	171	57	96	32	300
6. Kozyr E. N.	49	16.1	23	7.6	232	76.3	119	39.1	185	60.9	44	14.4	130	42.8	130	42.8	304
7. Fiodorov P. S.	85	21.3	17	4.2	298	74.5	233	58.3	167	41.7	37	9.2	215	53.8	148	37	400
the average speech-genre index	529	18.1	195	6.7	2,193	75.2	1,185	40.6	1,732	59.4	291	10	1,532	52.5	1,094	37.5	2,917

Table 6: Speech behaviour of the group of English-speaking public prosecutors at the beginning of the twenty-first century before a trial by jury

strategy / addressers	Participation/Nonparticipation of members of communication in a speech event						Sure/Unsure speech behaviour of an author				The sender's formation of addressee's attitude to a speech event by evaluation						MSG
	the plane of **personal** participation		the plane of **social** participation		the plane of **objective** participation		**certain** statement		**uncertain** statement		the plane of **positive** attitude		the plane of **neutral** attitude		the plane of **negative** attitude		
	MSG	%	MSG	%	MSG	%	MSG	%	MSG	%	MSG	%	MSG	%	MSG	%	
1. Templeman	66	14.9	48	10.8	330	74.3	312	70.3	132	29.7	86	19.4	252	56.7	106	23.9	444
2. Andrade	87	22.3	18	4.6	285	73.1	105	26.9	285	73.1	69	17.7	207	53.1	114	29.2	390
3. Dennis	64	15.8	12	3	328	81.2	76	18.8	328	81.2	36	8.9	232	57.4	136	33.7	404
4. Reid	44	10.3	20	4.7	362	85	38	8.9	388	91.1	22	5.2	306	71.8	98	23	426
5. Whylie	42	9.3	48	10.7	360	80	60	13.3	390	86.7	54	12	278	61.8	118	26.2	450
6. Smith	60	9.5	17	2.7	555	87.8	70	11.1	562	88.9	76	12	424	67.1	132	20.9	632

7. Kingston	59	13.1	27	6	364	80.9	90	20	360	80	57	12.7	276	61.3	117	26	450
the average speech-genre index	422	13.2	190	5.9	2584	80.9	751	23.5	2,445	76.5	400	12.5	1,975	61.8	821	25.7	3,196

Table 7: Stereotyped speech behaviour of prosecutors' groups

strategy / period / kind of trial / country	Participation/Nonparticipation of members of communication in a speech event						Sure/Unsure speech behaviour of an author				The sender's formation of addressee's attitude to a speech event by evaluation						MSG
	the plane of **personal** participation		the plane of **social** participation		the plane of **objective** participation		**certain** statement		**uncertain** statement		the plane of **positive** attitude		the plane of **neutral** attitude		the plane of **negative** attitude		
	MSG	%	MSG	%	MSG	%	MSG	%	MSG	%	MSG	%	MSG	%	MSG	%	
1. the end of the XIX century / trial by jury / Russia	624	12.4	384	7.6	3,986	80	2,119	42.4	2,875	57.6	547	11	2,298	46	2,149	43	4,994
2. 20s-40s years of the XX century / professional trial/ USSR	482	10	652	13.6	3,659	76.4	2,086	43.5	2,707	56.5	684	14.3	1,723	35.9	2,386	49.8	4,793

3. XXI century / professional trial / Russia	1,678	31.2	39	0.7	3,660	68.1	3,017	56.1	2,360	43.9	631	11.8	1,620	30.1	3,126	58.1	5,377
4. XXI century / trial by jury / Russia	529	18.1	195	6.7	2,193	75.2	1,185	40.6	1,732	59.4	291	10	1,532	52.5	1,094	37.5	2,917
5. XXI century / trial by jury / Great Britain	422	13.2	190	5.9	2,584	80.9	751	23.5	2,445	76.5	400	12.5	1,975	61.8	821	25.7	3,196
the average speech-genre index	3,735	17.5	1,460	6.9	16,082	75.6	9,158	43	12,119	57	2,553	12	9,148	43	9,576	45	21,277

WORKS CITED

Adcock, C. J. Fundamentals of Psychology. Aulesbury: Pelican,1964.

Agapova, S. G. Osobennosti rechevogo povedeniya adresanta i adresata // Aktualnie problemi metodiki prepodavahiya russkogo yazika kak inostrannogo. Rostov-on-Don, 2002.

Ageeva, Z. A. Lichnost kak obyekt psikhologicheskogo vozdeystviya // Psikhologicheskoe vozdeystviye na lichnost i gruppu. – Ivanovo, 1989.

Aleksandrov, D. N. Ritorika. M., 1993.

Alekseev, A. I. Yastrebov V. B. Professiya prokuror. M., 1998.

Andreev, V. I. Delovaya ritorika. Kazan, 1993.

Antonenko, T. A. Slovesnost v yurisprudentsii. Rostov-on-Don, 1999.

Apresyan, G. Z. Oratorskoye iskusstvo. M., 1969.

Arotser, L. E. Taktika i etika sudebnogo doprosa. M., 1999.

Arutyunova, N. D. Pragmatika // Yazykoznaniye. Bolshoi entsiklopedicheskiy slovar / Gl. red. V. N. Yartseva. M., 2000.

Aseeva, Zh. V. Lexicheskiye sredstva vyrazheniya ideologii politicheskoy korrektnosti v sovremennom angliyskom yazyke. Avtoref. dis. … kand. filol. nauk. Irkutsk, 1999.

Bach, K. "Speech Acts." In Routledge Encyclopedia of Philosophy. London: Routledge, 1998.

Baeva, O. A. Oratorskoe iskusstvo i delovoe obshchenie. Минск, 2000.

Bagdassarian, T. M. Rechevoe povedenie vrachey-psihkoterapevtov (na materiale angliyskogo i russkogo yazykov). Avtoref. dis. … kand. filol. nauk. Rostov-on-Don, 2004.

Bakhtin, M. M. Problema rechevih zhanrov // Literaturno-kriticheskiye statyi. M., 1986.

Baskov, V. I. Na sudebnoy tribune—gosudarstvenniy obvinitel // Sovetskaya prokuratura. Istoriya i sovremennost. M., 1977.

Baskov, V. I. Prokuror v sude pervoy instantsii. M., 1968.

—. Prokurorskiy nadzor za ispolneniem zakonov pri rassmotrenii ugolovnih del v sudah. M., 1986.

Bazylev, V. N. Belchikov, Yu. A. Leontiev, A. A. Sorokin, Yu. A. Kak slovo nashe otzoviotsia. – http://jude.lawmix.ru/comm/8075/

Belyaeva, A. V. Korotkov V. L. Tarabrina N. V. Lichnotsniy aspect verbalnogo vzaimodeystviya v diade // Psikhologicheskie issledovaniya obshcheniya. M., 1985.

Beria, S. Moi otets - Lavrentiy Beria. http://www.duel.ru/publish/beria/beria.html

Berman, H. *Justice in the USSR*. New York: Vintage, 1963.

Bodaliov, A. A. Lichnost i obshchenie. M., 1995.

Bolshoi, anglo-russkiy slovar / Pod red. I. R. Galperina i E. M. Mednikovoy. M., 1988.

Boyko, V. V. Metodi intellektualnogo vozdeystviya na slushateley lektsii // Psikhologicheskoye vozdeystviye na lichnost i gruppu. Ivanovo, 1989.

Butussova, A. S. Pragmaticheskiy potentsial ellipticheskih predlozheniy. Diss. … kandidata filol. nauk. Rostov-on-Don, 2003.

Cambridge Advanced Learner's Dictionary. http://dictionary.cambridge.org/dictionary/british/pessimism

Charleston, B. *Studies in the Emotional and Affective Means of Expression in Modern English*. Bern, 1960.

Chayka I. Khitrosti Public Relations. http://www.7st.ru/articles.phtml?id=23

Cheremissin, P. G. Posobiye po stilistike russkogo yazika. M., 1971.

Chernoivanova, O. I. K voprosu kategorii neuverennosti kak pragmalingvisticheskoy kharakteristiki pozhilogo cheloveka // Lichnost, rech i yuridicheskaya praktika. Vypusk 1. Rostov-on-Don, 1998.

Chigridova, N. Yu. Kholodkova L. K. Strategiya sotsialnogo prestizha v rechi delovogo kommunikanta // Lichnost, rech i yuridicheskaya praktika. Vypusk 4. Rostov-on-Don, 2001.

Chigridova, N. Yu. Opredeleniye lingvisticheskikh aktualizatorov strategii sotsialnogo prestizha // Filologiya v obrazovatelnom prostranstve donskogo regiona i eyo rol v razvitii lichnosti. Vypusk 4. Rostov-on-Don, 2001.

Chufarovskiy, Yu. V. Yuridicheskaya psikhologiya. M., 1995.

Chuldini, R. Psikhologiya vliyaniya. http://antisectik.narod.ru/soz_psi/soz_reflex.htm

Chunakhova, L. V. Osobennosti rechevogo povedeniya khudozhnikov vtoroy polovini XIX veka (na materiale angliyskogo i russkogo yazikov). Diss. … kandidata filol. nauk. Rostov-on-Don, 2006.

Danilevich, A. A. Sudebnie preniya i ikh mesto v sisteme sudebnogo razbiratelstva ugolovnikh del. Kiev, 1991.

Dementyev, V. V. Izucheniye rechevikh zhanrov: obzor rabot v sovremennoy rusistike // Voprossi yazikoznaniya 1, 1997.

Dilts, Robert. Fokussi yazika: Izmeneniye ubezhdeniy s pomoshchyu NLP. SPb, 2001.

Dodonov, B. I. Emotsiya kak tsennost. M., 1978.

—. V mire emotsiy. Kiev: Politizdat Ukraini, 1987.

Drugaliova, E. V. Poniatie rechevogo zhanra v sovremennoy lingvistike // Problemi rossiyskoy pravovoy sistemi. Taganrog, 2003.

Egorova, M. S. Psikhologiya individualnikh razlichiy. M., 1997.

Egorshina, E. E. Pragmalingvisticheskie osobennosti lexicheskikh usiliteley v sovremennom nemetskon yazike. Diss. … kandidata filol. nauk. Rostov-on-Don, 1997.

Ekzempliarov, R. Forma polemiki v sude // Sots. Zakonnost 4, 1976.

Enikeev, M. I. Entsiklopediya. Obshchaya i sotsialnaya psikhologiya. – M., 2002.

—. Osnovi obshchey i yuridicheskoy psikhologii. M., 1996.

Eysenck, H. J. *The structure of human personality*. New York, 1953.

Faydysh, E. A. Informatsionnaya organizatsiya psikhologicheskogo vozdeystviya // Psikhologiya vozdeystviya. M., 1989.

Federalniy, zakon "O prokurature Rossiyskoy Federatsii" ot 17.11.1995, №168 – FZ // Sbornik zakonov Rossiyskoy Federatsii / Pod obshchey red. Yu. N. Vlassova. M., 2000.

Fiodorova, L. L. Tipologiya rechevogo vozdeystviya i ego mesto v structure obshcheniya // Voprosi yazikoznaniya 6, 1991.

Formanovskaya, N. I. Rechevoy etiket i kultura obshcheniya. M., 1989.

Foss, D. J., Hakes D.T. *Psycholinguistics: An Introduction to the Psychology of Language*. New Jersey: prentice Hall, 1978.

Gamble, Teri Kwal, Michael Gamble. *Communication Works*. New York: McGraw-Hill Higher Education, 1990.

Gasparov, B. M. Yazik, pamiat, obraz. Lingvistika yazikovogo sushchestvovaniya. M., 1996.

Goffman, E. *Relations in public—Microstudies of the Public Order*. London: Basic Books, 1971.

Golanova, E. I. Ustnaya publichnaya rech. Zhanr publichnoy lektsii // Russkiy yazik v ego funktsionirovanii. Kommunikativno-pragmaticheskiy aspect. M., 1993.

Golev, N. D. Yuridicheskiy aspect yazika v lingvisticheskom osveshchenii // Yurislingvistika. Problemi i perspektivi. Barnaul, 1999.

Gorlo, E. A. Pragmaticheskoe diagnostirovanie rechevogo povedeniya avtorov poeticheskikh textov (na materiale russkoy i nemetskoy poezii). Diss. … kandidata filol. nauk. Rostov-on-Don, 2004.

Grice, H. P. "Logic and Conversation." In *Syntax and Semantics* volume 3, edited by Peter Cole and Jerry L. Morgan, 41–58. New York: Academic Press, 1975.

Gvozdev, A. N. Ocherki po stilistike russkogo yazika. – M., 1965.

Hall, Calvin S., Lindzey Gardner. Teorii lichnosti (Theories of Personality). M., 1997.
Hornby, A.S. *Oxford Advanced Learner's Dictionary of Current English*; Cowie A. P. London: Oxford University Press, 1974.
—. Oxford progressive English for adult learners. London: Oxford University Press ,1994.
Ivakina, N. N. Kultura sudebnoy rechi. M., 1995.
—. Osnovi sudebnogo krasnorechiya (ritorika dlia yuristov). M., 2000.
Ivin, A. A. Osnovaniya logiki otsenok. M., 1970.
—. Ritorika: iskusstvo ubezhdat. M., 2002.
Istoria gosudarstva i prava zarubezhnikh stran. Chast 2. Pod red.
Karasik, V. I. Etnokulturnie tipi institutsionalnogo diskursa // Etnokulturnaya spetsifika rechevoy deyatelnosti. M., 2000.
Khanin, Yu. L. O kriteriyakh effektivnosti psikhologicheskikh vozdeystviy // Psikhologicheskoe vozdeystviye na lichnost i gruppu. – Ivanovo, 1989.
Khazagerov, G. G. Politicheskaya ritorika: s chego nachat? – http://evartist.narod.ru/text7/11.htm
Kisseleva, L. A. Voprosi teorii rechevogo vozdeystviya. L., 1978.
Kjell, L., Ziengler, D. Teoriya lichnosti - Theory of personality (Osnovnie polozheniya, issledovaniya i primeneniye). SPb., 1997.
Kochkin, M. Yu. O manipuliatsii v sovremennom politicheskom diskurse // http://tpl1999.narod.ru/WebStud1/SbornikSt1-1.htm.
Kokhtev, N. N. Ritorika. M., 1994.
Koni, A. F. Kniaz A. I. Urussov i F. N. Plevako // Poln. sobr. soch., t.5, 1968.
Koni, A. F. Vospominaniya o dele Veri Zasulich // Poln. sobr. soch., t.2, 1968.
Koshelyuk, M. Printsip PR – Proiskhozhdeniye. http://www.princippr.ru/proish/boss-kniga-ch3.htm
Kovaliov, G. A. O sisteme psikhologicheskogo vozdeystviya // Psikhologiya vozdeystviya. – M., 1989.
Krasheninnikovoy, N. A., Zhidkova O. A. – M., 1998.
Kvashis, V. E. Smertnaya kazn I obshchestvennoe mnenie // Gosudarstvo i pravo 4, 1997.
Kravchenko, S. Uchastie prokurora v sudebnom razbiratelstve ugolovnikh del. http://tarasei.narod.ru/dip/duchp.htm
Kryssin, L. P. Rechevoe obshchenie i sotsialnie roli govoriashchikh // Sotsialno-lingvisticheskie issledovaniya. M., 1976.
Kucherena, A. Nizko prestuplenie, a chelovek dostoin sozhaleniya. Tri grekha rossiyskoy prokuraturi.

http://www.rg.ru/anons/arc_2000/0422/1.htm

Kunitsina, V. N. Kazarinova N. V. Pogolsha V. M. Mezhlichnostnoe obshchenie. SPb., 2002.

Leech, G.N. Principles of Pragmatics. London, 1985.

Lenets, A. V. Pragmalingvisticheskaya diagnostika osobennostey rechevogo povedeniya nemetskogo uchitelia. Avtoref. dis. ... kand. filol. nauk. Piatigorsk, 1999.

—. Pragmaticheskiy aspect aktsentirovaniya elementov vyskazivaniya // Lichnost, rech i yuridicheskaya praktika. Vyp. 4. Rostov-on-Don, 2001. Leongard K. Aktsentuirovannie lichnosti. Kiev, 1981.

Leontiev, A. A. Psikhologicheskie i psikholingvisticheskie problemi vladeniya i ovladeniya yazykom. – M., 1969.

—. Osnovi psikholingvistiki. M.: Smysl, 1999.

Leontiev, A. N. Motivi, emotsii i lichnost // Psikhologiya lichnosti. Teksti. Pod red. Yu. B. Gippenreyter, A. A. Puzyreya. M., 1982.

—. Potrebnosti, motivi, emotsii // Psikhologiya emotsiy. Texti / Pod red. V. K. Vilyunasa, Yu. B. Gippenreyter. M., 1984.

Lichko, A. E. Psikhopatii I aktsentuatsii kharaktera u podrostkov. L., 1983.

Likas, A. L. Kultura pravosudiya. M., 1990.

—. Kultura sudebnogo protsessa. M., 1971.

Lomov, B. F. Problemi i strategiya psikholingvisticheskogo issledovaniya // Ros. akad. nauk, In-t psikhologii. M., 1999.

Lomova, O. E. Rechevoe povedeniye aktiorov v avtobiograficheskikh textakh (na materiale russkogo i nemetskogo yazikov). Diss. ... kandidata filol. nauk. – Rostov-on-Don, 2004.

Longman Dictionary of Contemporary English. Harlow: Longman, 1995.

Longman Dictionary of English Idioms. Harlow and London: Longman, 1980.

Longman Dictionary of English Language and Culture. Harlow: Longman, 1992.

Lye, J. "Jakobson′s Communication Model."
http://www.brocku.ca/commstudies/courses/2F50/jakobson.html

Mac, Cann D. *How to Influence Others at Work: Psychoverbal Communication for Managers.* London: Heinemann Professional, 1988.

Mackenzie, W. J. M. *Biological Ideas in Politics: An Essay in Political Adaptivity*. Manchester: Penguin, 1979.

Magun, V. S. Potrebnosti i psikhologiya sotsialnoy deyatelnosti lichnosti. L., 1983.

Makarenko, V. P. Byurrokratiya I stalinizm. Rostov-on-Don, 1989.

Makarov, M. L. Interpretativniy analiz diskursa v maloy gruppe. Tver, 1998.

Makarova, Z. V. Oratorskoe iskusstvo v sude. L., 1985.

Maslow, A. H. *Hierarchy of Needs: A Theory of Human Motivation*. New York: Harper, 1954.

—. A Theory of Metamotivation: The Biological Rooting of the Value Life // Journal of Humanistic Psychology 7 (1967): 93–127.

—. Motivation and personality. New York: Harper, 1954.

Massarskiy, M. V. Ubezhdayushchee slovo. M., 1979.

Matveeva, G. G. Aktualizatsiya pragmaticheskogo aspecta nauchnogo texta. Rostov-on-Don, 1984.

—. Diagnostirovanie lichnostnikh svoystv avtora po ego rechevomu povedeniyu. Rostov-on-Don, 1998.

—. K metodike analiza texta v aspecte skrytoy pragmalingvistiki // Edinitsi yazika: funktsionalno-kommunikativniy aspect. Chast 2. Rostov-on-Don, 2001.

—. K voprosu o skrytom vozdeystvii otpravitelia nauchnogo texta na ego poluchatelia // Grammatiko-stilisticheskie osobennosti yazikovikh edinits v texte (na materiale romanskikh I germanskikh yazikov). Saratov, 1990.

—. Osnovi kulturi ustnoy rechi. Rostov-on-Don, 1997.

—. Skrytie grammaticheskie znacheniya I identifikatsiya sotsialnogo litsa ("portreta") govoriashchego. Diss. … doktora filol. nauk. SPb., 1993.

—. Sopostavlenie informativnikh i funktsionalnikh sem pri issledovanii semanticheskoy strukturi glagola // Sopostavitelniy analiz lingvisticheskikh kategoriy. Tomsk, 1985.

—. Strategicheskie plani pragmaticheskogo soderzhaniya texta // Mezhvuz. sb. nauchn. trudov. M., 1986.

Matveeva, G. G. Nuzhnova E. E. Tonchenko L. N. Malaya sintaksicheskaya gruppa kak edinitsa pragmaticheskogo issledovaniya // Aktualnie problemi filologii I metodiki prepodavaniya. Ch. 1. Rostov-on-Don, 2001.

Melnik, V. V. Iskusstvo dokazivaniya v sostiazatelnom ugolovnom protsesse. M., 2000.

Mikhailovskaya, N. G. Odintsov V. V. Iskusstvo sudebnogo oratora. M., 1981.

Mikhaylov, M. M. Stilistika russkoy rechi. Cheboksari, 1968.

Mikhlin, A. Evolyutsiya zakonodatelstva o primenenii smertnoy kazni // Zakonnost 4, 1997.

Mkrtchyan, T. Yu. Rechevoe povedenie zhurnalistov v politicheskom tele- i radiointervyu (na materiale russkogo I angliyskogo yazikov). Diss. … kandidata filol. nauk. Rostov-on-Don, 2004.

Moiseenko, L. A. Rechevoe povedenie avtorov voennikh memuarov i diagnostirovanie ikh individualnikh svoystv (na materiale nemetskogo yazika). Avtoref. dis. … kand. filol. nauk. Piatigorsk, 2000.

Myasishchev, V. N. Lichnost i nevrozi. L., 1960.

—. O vzaimosviazi obshcheniya, otnosheniya i otrazheniya kak probleme obshchey i sotsialnoy psikhologii // Sotsialno-psikhologicheskaya i lingvisticheskaya kharakteristiki obshcheniya i razvitiya kontaktov mezhdu lyudmi. L., 1970.

Nastolnaya kniga prokurora / Pod red. Gerasimova S. I. M., 2002.

Nayer, V. L. Pragmatika texta I eyo sostavliayushchie // Pragmaticheskiy aspect predlozheniya i texta. L., 1990.

Nazarov, N. V. O sintagmatike poslovits kak rechevogo zhanra // Funktsionirovaniye yazika v razlichnikh rechevikh zhanrakh. Vypusk IV. Limanchik, 1997.

Nozhin, E. A. Osnovi sovetskogo oratorskogo iskusstva. M., 1973.

Nuzhnova, E. E. Нужнова E.E. Pragmalingvisticheskiy aspect rechevogo povedeniya spetsialistov v oblasti kompyuternoy tekhniki. Diss. … kandidata filol. nauk. Rostov-on-Don, 2003.

Orlov, A. V. Smertnaya kazn // Yurist, 1, 1999.

Ozhegov, S. I. Slovar russkogo yazika. M., 1997.

Panicheva, A. I. Sudebnaya rech // Prokurorskiy nadzor. June 6, 2003. http://www.memo.ru/hr/refugees/sem10rus/Chapter11.htm

Pavlova, L. G. Nravstvennaya pozitsiya govoriashchego // Edinitsi yazika: funktsionalno-kommunikativniy aspect. Chast 2. Rostov-on-Don, 2001.

Petrenko, V. F. Psikhosemantika soznaniya. M., 1988.

Piotrovskiy, R. G. Ocherki po stilistike frantsuzskogo yazika. L., 1960.

Pirinova, N. V. Elementi khudozhestvennogo stilya v sudebnoy literature dorevolyutsionnogo perioda // Edinitsi yazika: funktsionalno-kommunikativniy aspect. Chast 2. Rostov-on-Don, 2001.

Pocheptsov, G. G. Profession: image-maker. SPb., 2001.

Podgolin, E. E. O stile sudebnoy rechi // Sov. Yustitsiya 20, 1981. Porubov N. I. Ritorika. Minsk, 2001.

Prokurori i advokati: Znamenitiye protsessi / Sost. V. A. Kashevskiy, V. V. Moroz. Minsk, 1998.

Psikhologiya. Slovar. / Pod obsh. Red. A. V. Petrovskogo, M. G. Yaroshevskogo. M., 1990.

Pushkina, T. P. Meditsinskaya psikhologiya. Novosibirsk, 1996.

Puzyriov, A. V. Mnogoaspectnost funktsionirovaniya yazika v razlichnikh rechevikh zhanrakh // Funktsionirovaniye yazika v razlichnikh rechevikh zhanrakh. Vypusk IV. Limanchik, 1997.
Razinkina, N. M. Stilistika angliyskoy nauchnoy rechi. M., 1972.
Rechi izvestnikh russkikh yuristov. Predisloviye / Sost.: Zakharov P. M. M., 1985.
Rogov, E. I. Lichnost v pedagogicheskoy deyatelnosti. Rostov-on-Don, 1994.
Rokhlin, V. I. Dvorianskiy A. M. Organizatsiya i metodika uchastiya prokurora v rassmotrenii sudami ugolovnikh del. SPb., 1994.
Romanov, V. V. Yuridicheskaya psikhologiya. M., 2001.
Rossiyskoe, zakonodatelstvo X - XX vekov. V deviati tomakh. T.8. Sudebnaya reforma. – M., 1991.
Rowe, A. "Personality Theory and Behavioural Genetics: Contributions and Issues." In Personality Psychology: Recent Trends and Emerging Directions, edited by D.M. Buss and N. Carter. New York: Springer, 1989.
Rozin, V. M. Psikhologiya dlia yuristov. M., 1997.
Rubinshtein, S. L. Osnovi obshchey psikhologii. SPb., 1999.
Sapir, E. Izbrannie trudi po yazikoznaniyu i kulturologii. Э. M., 1993.
Saussure, F. Zapiski po obshchey lingvistike. M., 1990.
Savitskiy, A. N. Gosudarstvennoe obvinenie v sude. M., 1971.
Savyuk, L. K. Pravookhranitelnie organi. M., 2001.
Senkevich, M. P. Stilistika nauchnoy rechi i literaturnoe redaktirovanie nauchnikh proizvedeniy. M., 1976.
Sergeich, P. (Porokhovshchikov P. S.) Iskusstvo rechi na sude. M., 1988.
Sheinov, V. P. Skrytoe upravleniye chelovekom (Psikhologiya manipulirovaniya). Minsk, 2001.
Shikhantsov, G. G. Yuridicheskaya psikhologiya. M., 1998.
Ekzempliarov, R. Forma polemiki v sude // Sots. Zakonnost 4, 1976.
Solomon, P. Sovetskaya yustitsiya pri Staline. M., 1988.
Stepanov, S. S. Yazik i vneshnost. M., 2003.
Stepanov, Yu. S. V poiskakh pragmatiki (problema subyekta) // Izv. AS USSR, Ser. yaz. i lit., t. 40, 1981, №4.
Sternin, I. A., a. O natsionalnom kommunikativnom soznanii. – http://sternin.adeptis.ru/articles_rus.html
—. b. Rechevoe vozdeystvie kak integralnaya nauka. – http://sternin.adeptis.ru/articles_rus.html
—. c. Mozhno li kulturno formirovat kulturu v svremennoy Rossii? – http://sternin.adeptis.ru/articles_rus.html

Sutherland, J. "Role of the Prosecutor: A Brief History." Criminal Lawyers Association. http://dsp-psd.pwgsc.gc.ca/Collection-R/LoPBdP/BP/prb0211-e.htm

Tannen, D. "Discourse Analysis." http://bank.rug.ac.be/da/da.htm#et

Tarassov, E. F. Rechevoe vozdeystvie kak problema rechevogo obshcheniya. M., 1990.

Tarassov, G. S. O nepovtorimosti chelovecheskoy lichnosti // Voprosi psikhologii 3, 1989.

Tornaev, N. N. Tekhnika lichnoy raboti prokurora. M., 1999.

Tsariov, V. I. Struktura i stil sudebnoy rechi prokurora // Sots. Zakonnost, 4, 1983.

Uznadze, D. N. Motivatsionniy period, predshestvuyushchiy volevomu aktu // Psikhologiya lichnosti. Texti / Pod red. Yu. B. Gippenreyter, A. A. Pusyreya. – M., 1982. – C. 80-86.

Varnavskikh, N. V. Illokutivnie akti v zashchititelnoy rechi // Aktualnie problemi metodiki prepodavaniya russkogo yazika kak inostrannogo. Rostov-on-Don, 2002.

—. Pragmaticheskie ozhidaniya poluchatelia // Aktualnie problemi filologii i metodiki prepodavaniya. Chast I. Rostov-on-Don, 2001.

—. Tipologicheskie cherti pechevogo povedeniya russko - i anglogovoriashchikh advokatov (pragmalingvisticheskiy podkhod). Diss. ... kandidata filol. nauk. Rostov-on-Don, 2004.

Vassilyeva, I. I. O znachenii idey M. M. Bakhtina o dialoge I dialogicheskikh otnosheniyakh dlia psikhologii obshcheniya // Psikhologicheskiye issledovaniya obshcheniya / Otv. red. B. F. Lomov. M., 1985.

Vvvedenskaya, L. A. Pavlova L. G. Chikhachiov V. P. Kultura i tekhnika rechi. Rostov-on-Don, 1994.

Vinokur, T. G. Russkiy yazik v ego funktsionirovanii: kommunikativno-pragmaticheskiy aspect. M., 1993.

Vitsin, S. Vremia kaznit v Rossii zakonchilos? // Rossiyskaya yustitsiya 3, 1999.

Volk, S. Vydrya M. Muratov A. Anatoliy Fiodorovich Koni // Poln. sobr. soch., t.1.

Volkov, A. A. Kurs russkoy ritoriki. M., 2001.

Volkodaev, N. F. Pravovaya kultura sudebnogo protsessa. M., 1980.

Volodina, S. I. Psikhologicheskie i eticheskie osobennosti zashchititelnoy rechi. http://bestlawyers.ru/pub/pub8.html

Volf, E. M. Otsenochnoe znachenie I sootnoshenie priznakov "khorosho" "plokho" // Voprossi yazikoznaniya 5, 1986.

Vydrya, M. M. A. F. Koni kak sudebniy orator // A. F. Koni. Poln. sobr. soch., t. 3, 1967.

Wainwright, G. Yazik tela (Body Language). M., 1999.

Wheeler, M. *The Oxford Russian-English Dictionary*. Oxford: Oxford University Press, 1984.

Zagorskiy, G. N. Sudebnoe razbiratelstvo po ugolovnomu delu. M., 1998.

Zaitsev, S. I. Nikolay Vassilyevich Krylenko // Sovetskaya prokuratura. Istoria i sovremennost. M., 1977.

Zaychik, L. M. Uchastie prokurora v sudebnom razbiratelstve ugolovnih del M., 1970.

Zinchenko, V. P. Posokh Osipa Mandelshtama i Trubkas Mamardshvili. K nachalam organicheskoy psikhologii. M., 1997.

Zubarev, S. K. Yazik i stil obvinitelnogo zaklyucheniya. M., 1996.

Zvyagintsev, A. G. Prigovoryonnie vremenem: Rossiyskie i sovetskie prokurori: XX vek, 1937–1953 gg. M., 2001.

Zvyagintsev, A. G. Orlov Yu. G. Zhizn i deyaniya general-prokurorov Rossii v stsenakh i zarisovkakh. M., 2001.

Zyubina, I. A. Pragmalingvisticheskiy aspect rechevogo povedeniya russkogovoriashchego i anglogovoriashchego gosudarstvennogo obvinitelia. Diss. … kandidata filol. nauk. Rostov-on-Don, 2005.

—. Transformatsiya kak odno iz sredstv sozdaniya expressii gazetnikh zagolovkov // Edinitsi yazika: funktsionalno-kommunikativniy aspect. Chast 2. Rostov-on-Don, 2001.

LIST OF THE SPEECHES

Abramov N. V. Obvinitelnaya rech // Podderzhaniye gosudarstvennogo obvineniya v sude s uchastiyem prisiazhnikh zasedateley / Pod red. S. I. Gerassimova. – M., 2002. – P. 327 - 337.

Agapov R. V. Speeches for the prosecution // Records of judicial proceedings (Kirovskiy District Court, Rostov-on-Don).

Andrade Q.C. Speeches for the prosecution. – http://www.hrothgar.co.uk/WebCases/pc/frames/00/37.htm

Baev V. N. Speeches for the prosecution // Records of judicial proceedings (Kirovskiy District Court, Rostov-on-Don).

Dennis R. Speeches for the prosecution. – http://www.hrothgar.co.uk/WebCases/pc/frames/00/37.htm

Fedorin I. V. Speeches for the prosecution // Records of judicial proceedings (Kirovskiy District Court, Rostov-on-Don).

Fiodorov P. S. Obvinitelnaya rech // Podderzhaniye gosudarstvennogo obvineniya v sude s uchastiyem prisiazhnikh zasedateley / Pod red. S. I. Gerassimova. – M., 2002. – P. 369 - 378.

Glyuzitskiy A. V. Speeches for the prosecution // Records of judicial proceedings (Kirovskiy District Court, Rostov-on-Don).

Kazarinov M. G. Delo Pyevtsevich // Rechi izvestnikh russkikh yuristov / Sost.: Zakharov P. M. – M., 1985. – P. 196 - 201.

Kingston. Speeches for the prosecution. – http://www.hrothgar.co.uk/WebCases/pc/frames/00/39.htm

Kon F. N. Obvinitelnaya rech // Sudebniye rechi sovetskikh obviniteley. Sudebniye rechi sovetskikh obviniteley. Sbornik / Sost.: Alexandrov G. N., Finn E. A. – M., 1965. – P. 88 - 102.

Kondakov A. Rech prokurora Alexandra Kondakova. – http://www.bellona.no/ru/index.html

Kondrushkin I. S. Delo po obvineniyu vziatochnikov i raskhititeley na transporte // Sudebniye rechi sovetskikh obviniteley. Sudebniye rechi sovetskikh obviniteley. Sbornik / Sost.: Alexandrov G. N., Finn E. A. – M., 1965. – P. 104 - 118.

Koni A. F. Obvinitelnaya rech po "Delu o podloge zaveshchaniya kapitana gvardii Sedkova" // Koni A. F. Poln. sobr. sochineniy. T. 3. – M., 1967. – P. 307 - 334.

Kozyr E. N. Obvinitelnaya rech // Podderzhaniye gosudarstvennogo obvineniya v sude s uchastiyem prisiazhnikh zasedateley / Pod red. S. I. Gerassimova. – M., 2002. – P. 355 - 361.

Krassikov P. A. Obvinitelnaya rech // Sudebniye rechi sovetskikh obviniteley. Sudebniye rechi sovetskikh obviniteley. Sbornik / Sost.: Alexandrov G. N., Finn E. A. – M., 1965. – P. 70 - 83.

Krylenko N. V. Sudebniye rechi. Izbrannoe. – M., 1964. – P. 61 - 80.

Lunacharskiy A. V. Delo pravykh esserov // Sudebniye rechi sovetskikh obviniteley. Sudebniye rechi sovetskikh obviniteley. Sbornik / Sost.: Alexandrov G. N., Finn E. A. – M., 1965. – P. 8 - 28.

Makhno N. V. Speeches for the prosecution // Records of judicial proceedings (Kirovskiy District Court, Rostov-on-Don).

Melnikov A. V. Obvinitelnaya rech // Podderzhaniye gosudarstvennogo obvineniya v sude s uchastiyem prisiazhnikh zasedateley / Pod red. S. I. Gerassimova. – M., 2002. – P. 361 - 369.

Muraviov N. V. Obvinitelnaya rech po “Delu 1-go marta”. – http://www.hrono.ru/dokum/1800dok/188103procuror.php

Plevako F. N. Delo Azbukinoy // Rechi izvestnikh russkikh yuristov / Sost.: Zakharov P. M. – M., 1985. – P. 310 - 316.

Plevako F. N. Delo Barteniova // Rechi izvestnikh russkikh yuristov / Sost.: Zakharov P. M. – M., 1985. – P. 344 - 362.

Pokrovskiy M. N. Delo pravikh eserov // Sudebniye rechi sovetskikh obviniteley. Sudebniye rechi sovetskikh obviniteley. Sbornik / Sost.: Alexandrov G. N., Finn E. A. – M., 1965. – P. 28 - 36.

Reid J. Speeches for the prosecution. – http://www.hrothgar.co.uk/WebCases/pc/frames/00/37.htm

Romanov V. I. Obvinitelnaya rech // Podderzhaniye gosudarstvennogo obvineniya v sude s uchastiyem prisiazhnikh zasedateley / Pod red. S. I. Gerassimova. – M., 2002. – P. 346 - 354.

Salnikov V. N. Obvinitelnaya rech // Podderzhaniye gosudarstvennogo obvineniya v sude s uchastiyem prisiazhnikh zasedateley / Pod red. S. I. Gerassimova. – M., 2002. – P. 337 - 346.

Shinkarov K. V. Speeches for the prosecution // Records of judicial proceedings (Kirovskiy District Court, Rostov-on-Don).

Smith. Speeches for the prosecution. – http://www.hrothgar.co.uk/WebCases/pc/frames/00/39.htm

Templeman. Speeches for the prosecution. – http://www.hrothgar.co.uk/WebCases/pc/frames/00/45.htm

Trukhanov G. V. Speeches for the prosecution // Records of judicial proceedings (Regional Court of Rostov-on-Don).

Trukhanov G. V. Newspaper articles // Private archive of Trukhanov G. V.
Urussov A. I. Delo Mironovicha // Rechi izvestnikh russkikh yuristov / Sost.: Zakharov P. M. – M., 1985. – P. 528 - 542.
Vyshinskiy A. J. Sudebniye rechi. – M., 1955.
Whylie O. - http://www.hrothgar.co.uk/WebCases/pc/frames/00/37.htm
Zhukov N. A. Obvinitelnaya rech prokurora Zhukova N. A. – http://juristy.ru/vip/jukov.htm.